SELL YOUR BUSINESS BY DESIGN
NOT BY DEFAULT

A guide to selling your business for more money

RICK J. KREBS, CPA

www.sourcedmediabooks.com

ISBN: 978-1-945431-20-3

Printed in the United States of America.

CONTENTS

INTRODUCTION

During the Summer of 2005, my partner and I sold our majority shares of Liberty Mortgage, a mortgage bank. I was the "thought guy" back then and thought I could handle anything. Since I "knew" what I was doing, I did not enlist the help of anyone. I did it all myself. After all, admitting I needed help showed weakness, and I didn't want to be weak.

A few months later, my partner and I found ourselves in an attorney's office enlisting his help to get us paid what was owed by the new owner. "Why didn't I get help?" I thought. "How could I be so stupid and not have planned better for the sale of my business?" The sale was a disaster, and the experience was awful.

When I became an M&A advisor, I vowed not to let the same horrible experience happen to other business owners that happened to me. This is the purpose of this book. I've packed into the pages over 27 years of experience and knowledge. The content is not from academia: It is from the school of hard knocks, with real-world examples of successes and failures, written to the savvy business owner who is selling his or her business—his or her baby, if you will. The business owner who wants to maximize the cash in his or her pocket with an optimal selling price and preemptive tax-saving strategy. The business owner who will take care of the employees who have been loyal for many years. The business owner who wants a successful sale and smooth transition, who can look back with pride after the sale and say, "I built that, and now it belongs to someone else who will continue my legacy."

HOW DO I PREPARE TO SELL MY BUSINESS?

CHAPTER 1

10 Questions Every Business Seller Needs Answered

This chapter covers 10 questions you absolutely need to have answered when considering the sale of your business. These are the most common questions sellers have asked me as they contemplate the sale of their business. With every answer, I will provide valuable insights that you will need to consider when selling your business.

Here are the 10 questions you need answered:

1. What about Confidentiality?
2. How Should I Conduct Business If I Am in the Process of Selling the Company?
3. Who Do I Get to Help Me?
4. Do I Need to Perform a Background Check on My Buyer?
5. Should I Delegate Some of the Selling Work to an Employee?
6. When Is the Sale of My Business Final?
7. What Timeline Can I Expect When I Am Selling My Business?
8. What If the Seller Is on the Lease after Closing?
9. Why Do Sellers Need to Carry a Note as Part of the Transaction?
10. What about Training the New Owner and Noncompete Agreements?

QUESTION 1: What about Confidentiality?

Confidentiality is a crucial element of every business sale. You will need to take extra precautions to ensure privacy is not breached. A good advisor will guide you through how to accomplish this. There are three primary things that should be kept confidential:

1 The fact that your business is for sale

2 Information you provide to the buyer about your business

3 Your "secret sauce" (i.e., information about your company that will only be shared after the money is in your bank account and the transaction has closed)

Keep Confidential: The Fact That Your Business Is for Sale

Keeping a lid on the fact that your business is for sale takes careful attention from you (the seller), the buyer, your M&A advisor, and everyone involved in the sales process. Certain precautions must be taken to ensure employees, customers, and competitors don't discover that your business is for sale.

Attorneys and CPAs representing you are bound by ethical standards of confidentiality, so they don't need to sign a nondisclosure agreement (NDA), but all of the other people who are involved should sign an NDA. A buyer or prospective buyer should sign an NDA before confidential information is provided to him or her. It is a common practice for an NDA to include the buyer and the buyer's advisors, who are all covered under the NDA signed by the buyer. Your M&A advisor will usually handle that, but if you are approached directly, then you will need to require the buyer to sign an NDA. There is an example of an NDA at the end of this book in the Appendix.

Unfortunately, I have experienced too many instances to count when a seller told me he or she had been approached by a potential buyer "out of the blue" who was interested in buying the seller's business. The seller, excited about the prospects of selling, let emotion overrule common sense and shared his or her tax returns and financials freely with this prospective buyer without having the buyer sign an NDA. Sometimes this is harmless, but it can also be deadly to your business.

One guerrilla tactic used by buyers you should be aware of—even if it is rarely done—is to pose as a real buyer, get your confidential information, then use it to destroy your business. Some of these "buyers" are your competitors. Make sure you give your M&A advisor a list of excluded people who can't see the information about your business before you take it to market. This will help alleviate, but won't wholly terminate, the threat of rogue buyers set to ruin your company.

Here is a word of caution about confidentiality: Sometimes, word gets out that your business is for sale no matter how hard you try to keep the secret. Maintaining the confidentiality of the transaction is a difficult task, and it can sometimes be breached, even by accident. Take every precaution to keep the transaction confidential, and be prepared to make a statement in case the news spreads. If the word does get out, here are some effective strategies for handling a confidentiality breach:

- Plan ahead so you know what you will say if you're asked by an employee or customer about selling your business.
- You should never lie about selling your business, but that doesn't mean you can't be vague and speak in generalities. You do not have to elaborate, but you will have to either substantiate or obliterate what the individual believes to be true. Ask questions to learn more before answering (e.g., "What have you heard? What makes you think that? Why would you think I'm selling?").
- You could respond to inquiries by saying, "Of course I would sell the business for the right price. Everything is for sale for the right price. Now go back to work!"
- For employees, lay it out for them and explain why you are selling and that you can't possibly stay and work forever. Tell them that you want to make sure they are being taken care of for their many years of service and promise that you won't choose a buyer who wants to come in and fire them. Explain that buyers, as a general rule, want to keep the employees happy since the employees are a valuable asset for the business. If the buyer bought a company and everyone quit, the buyer wouldn't have a company left.

- Tell them that you want to see the business succeed so it continues to create and maintain jobs for loyal employees. Explain that you are looking at ways to help with that growth, which includes finding a strong buyer who can take it to the next level.
- If people ask, tell them that even if the business sold, you wouldn't be going anywhere soon.
- Sometimes a buyer will offer key employees profit sharing, bonuses, and even options for ownership. Only tell this to a key employee who is confronting you about the sale.

Keep Confidential: Information You Provide to the Buyer about Your Business

As part of the sale, you will be sharing highly proprietary and confidential financial and operational information about your business. This is normal. Buyers are legally bound and expected to adhere to the NDA, which prohibits the sharing of this information with anyone besides their advisory team (who is also bound by the NDA). Although you don't have complete control of a buyer, you have legal remedies if the buyer breaches the NDA.

Generally, buyers are careful about protecting the confidentiality of information because breaching confidentiality can undermine the value and damage the business they are buying. For example, if you are purchasing a new car, you wouldn't intentionally scratch the paint in the showroom because it would devalue the vehicle. The same holds true with business buyers.

The confidential information is usually shared on the Cloud in a protected data room (like Dropbox), where it can be freely accessed by the buyer's advisors.

Keep Confidential: Your "Secret Sauce"

We all know about Kentucky Fried Chicken (KFC) and their secret chicken recipe. KFC's parent corporation told *The Chicago Tribune*, "We have a high-tech home for the Colonel's handwritten Original Recipe from 1940 here in our headquarters in Louisville, KY. It's stored in a secret vault in a digital safe that only a few people have access to and no one person can access it alone." To make sure the recipe remains a secret, it is "prepared by two different suppliers before being combined together and packaged for our restaurants" (Jay Jones, "Recipe remains company treasure," August 19, 2016).

Keeping their recipe a secret for so long is one of the reasons KFC has been so successful. Your business is much the same way. There are things that contribute to the success of your business that only a few people know. If you divulge these things (your "secret sauce") to a potential buyer, he or she can use the information against you to start a new company and compete against you.

I tell sellers all the time to be honest and direct, but don't give away your "secret sauce" (your "11 herbs and spices") until the transaction has closed and the money is in your bank. Examples of your own secret sauce may include recipes, marketing methods, manufacturing processes, trade secrets, proprietary information, and/or techniques for getting customers or winning contracts. You know what these differentiators are. Ask yourself, "What should I keep confidential about my business?" Don't share this before closing.

One item to note here is to NEVER give a buyer a list of your employees and customers until you feel comfortable that the buyer won't use or can't use that information against you. If you need to divulge key employee and customer names, be very careful. Consult with your advisor before making decisions about divulgence.

QUESTION 2: How Should I Conduct Business If I Am in the Process of Selling the Company?

The simple answer to this question is to keep conducting business as usual. Conduct business as if you are never going to sell it, for two reasons:

- It is easy to get so excited about the sale that you begin to neglect the business and sales decrease. If sales decrease, the buyer will be alarmed and want to pay you less for your business.
- The sale of your business may fall through.

Though easier said than done, running your business "as usual" is necessary for a successful sale. A critical aspect of this rule is capital expenditures (CAPEX), or any significant expenditure that you need to make between the time of signing the letter of intent (LOI) and closing. If your business is one that requires you to buy equipment to continue your growth pattern, you will need to address how to be compensated for the additional equipment purchased in the LOI. This can be negotiated with the buyer up front, but if mismanaged, it can be financially detrimental to you as the seller. I suggest that new equipment purchases increase the purchase price and that financing for new equipment should be assumed by the buyer. If it is addressed in the LOI, you get credit for these and don't get penalized for it.

A few years ago, I sold an equipment rental company. As part of the ongoing business model, the seller needed to buy generators to lease to customers periodically. Each generator cost between $60,000 and $100,000 but would generate enough revenue to pay for the purchase through the rental income in 12 months. The seller was hesitant to buy new generators at first because he wouldn't be compensated for them in the purchase price. He would lose money if he bought the generators that he needed to buy to keep the business going. He was in a quandary. The buyer, of course, didn't want the revenue to cease or stop climbing, so we negotiated in the LOI a provision that all new generators purchased between the time of the signing of the LOI and closing, once approved by the buyer, would increase the selling price of the business. Both the seller and the buyer were satisfied with this solution.

Unforeseen events sometimes occur during due diligence. Examples may include a significant customer filing for bankruptcy, the loss of a key employee, or loss of a key customer, product line, or service. If an event occurs that could impact future business operations, it is imperative that the buyer be notified as soon as possible and consulted about how to proceed. Buyers do NOT like to be lied to or strung along. This is damaging and could create a lawsuit. The last thing you want to do is sell your business and then end up in a court battle about the sale.

QUESTION 3: Who Do I Get to Help Me?

Like most business owners considering the sale of a business, you probably haven't sold a business before. You aren't sure where to turn for advice and help. Selling a business is a complex transaction that requires a team of professionals, not just one individual. Hiring a team of specialists is absolutely essential to ensure the most favorable outcome. This is such a crucial step of the process that I've devoted a whole chapter of this book (Chapter 23) to help you choose the right advisory team. This section will identify who these people are and the roles they play. Chapter 23 will tell you how to choose a winning team and give you a list of people to get started with.

In the world of selling businesses, we call true professional advisors "deal guys." Deal guys are a must— they are professionals who know how to get business sale transactions across the finish line. These are people who work in the space, have experience closing transactions, and get things done. They are professional, knowledgeable, and collaborative team players who work well with all of the members of the advisory team.

On the other hand, choosing the wrong people to be on your advisory team is one of the three biggest mistakes I see business owners make. Bad advisors kill transactions or increase pain and suffering, plain and simple. I have a word of caution as you consider who to hire: There are a significant number of people out there who want to practice law or accounting or who want to be an M&A advisor but have little or no experience. I call them apprentice advisors. They aren't afraid to take on an engagement to gain the experience on your dime. These people can quickly kill a sale before you know what happened. Chapter 23 of this book contains a list of trusted, vetted advisors I have worked with in the past. This is a good starting point for finding the right people to help you. You will need to hire at least three people to help you sell, including the following:

Transaction Attorney	Selling Advisor (business broker, M&A advisor, or investment banker)	Tax Attorney or Tax CPA

Transaction Attorney

Maneuvering the process of selling a business is a lot like swimming with sharks: At any time, you can get partially or totally eaten alive if you aren't careful. You need to have an attorney who has been through the process many times, specializes in mergers and acquisitions, and understands the laws involved.

An unfortunate example of this happened to me a few years ago. We were in the process of selling a business and almost through the contract phase of the transaction. When we signed the LOI, I asked the seller if he had an attorney who was experienced and knowledgeable about selling businesses. (I always ask this because I can recommend one if needed.) He said that he had an attorney, whom we used.

Going through the contracts one day, we were on a conference call that included the buyers, the buyers' legal team, the seller, and the seller's attorney. There was wording that needed to be added to the contract for a matter we were negotiating. The seller's attorney kept objecting to adding the wording. The wording wasn't unusual as it pertained to the sale of a business, so I asked if the seller's attorney and I could have a minute on our side to discuss how to handle the matter.

I put the phone on hold and asked the seller's attorney to add the wording to this contract from another transaction she had done so we could move on. The attorney looked at me in a funny way and told me she had never handled a business sale before. She was a divorce attorney. She didn't have the wording to add in her file.

I could have fainted then and there. I couldn't believe we had come that far and she wasn't qualified to represent the seller! Clumsily, we were able to close the transaction in spite of the divorce attorney, but I learned a valuable lesson: Get a transaction expert! The buyers later told me that if they ever had that happen again, they would give the seller a list of recommended attorneys to choose from or walk away from the transaction. The attorney could have cost the seller millions of dollars.

Selling Advisor: Business Broker, M&A Advisor, or Investment Banker

This next role needs to be filled by a professional who has experience selling businesses that are the same approximate size as your business.

This person, the selling advisor, will be the "quarterback" of your team. He or she will help you bring in other team members as necessary in a manner that will save you time and money. The selling advisor will be your confidant, trusted advisor, and emotional sounding board when things get rough. He or she will be critical for getting you the most money for your business. I can't count the number of times I've been told if I hadn't been there to keep things together, the sale wouldn't have occurred.

A selling advisor is extremely valuable throughout the sales process. I'm not saying that you can't sell your business without an advisor, because you can, but it wouldn't be pretty. (You can also do surgery on yourself, but that wouldn't be pretty either.) Spend the money and get a good advisor—he or she will either save or make you more money than he or she cost. Either way, the advisor is well worth the money.

Let your advisor be your sounding board. Explain your priorities so he or she can better help you get what you want out of the business sale. Give this team member the ability to negotiate with the buyer, and don't be afraid to use his or her expertise to maneuver the pathway to closing.

Recently, a seller told me how his transaction was such an emotional roller coaster ride that he constantly needed me to calm his nerves. At one point during the sales process, had he approached the buyer with his proposal, it would have killed his transaction. He needed a buffer to make the deal happen. Selling a business is a highly emotional process; raw nerves and no advisor as a buffer spell disaster. My friend Garrett Gunderson, author of *Killing Sacred Cows*, said it well: "The higher the emotion, the lower the intelligence" (Wealth Factory Wealth Summit, October 2, 2019).

Having a third-party person involved in the transaction can help move through the "sticky points," leaving the seller/buyer relationship intact after closing.

There are three tiers of selling advisors, each specializing in businesses of a certain size.

1. **Business Broker: business value < $1 million**
   Business brokers are good at handling the "main street" transactions. They specialize in the "mom and pop" businesses.

2. **Mergers and Acquisitions (M&A) Advisor:
$1 million < business value < $30 million**
M&A advisors fill a void left between the investment bankers and business brokers called the lower mid-market.
3. **Investment Bankers: business value > $30 million**
The investment bankers handle mid-market transactions.

Fees for the three types of advisors are as follows:

- Business brokers charge 10 to 12 percent of the transaction amount, a small amount up front (typically less than $2,500), and no monthly retainer.
- M&A advisors charge fees on a sliding scale from 5 to 10 percent of the transaction amount (depending on the size of the transaction), a small amount up front (typically less than $5,000), and no monthly retainer.
- Investment bankers charge fees on a sliding scale from 3 to 7 percent of the transaction amount (depending on the size of the transaction), plus a fee up front and monthly retainers.

Be cautious: If you are selling your business for less than $30 million, do not spend over $5,000 for an upfront appraisal. Here are two guerrilla tactics to be aware of that are sometimes used by brokers and M&A advisors:

1. Some firms charge between $30,000 and $50,000 for an upfront appraisal but then don't get the sale done because they already made their money.
2. Some brokers and advisors will tell you that they can get more for your business than what is realistic in order to secure the listing. You, as a seller, get excited, thinking this advisor must be better because he or she can get a higher price for your business. Once your business is listed, it usually sits on the market for a long period of time. Then, after making selling price cuts, it sells for what the market will bear. Getting an outside third-party valuation is a good idea to determine a realistic selling price.

Overall, the cost of selling a business is higher than the cost of selling a house or real estate due to the complexity of the transaction and the time required to complete the sale. You will find that the money you spend will be more than made up for by setting a higher selling price, using a tax-reduction strategy, or avoiding expensive litigation.

I had two sellers come to me months after we had closed on the sale of their business. We had carefully negotiated the wording of the purchase and sale agreement in their favor for tax purposes. The buyer was a large national company, yet the CEO wasn't aware of the impact of the structure we had so carefully worded in the contract in the seller's favor. He didn't care too much since it didn't significantly impact him, but it did substantially impact the seller in a positive manner. Had we not done what we did, the sellers would have had to pay hundreds of thousands of dollars more in taxes. There is no way the sellers would have known how to structure the sale as we did on their own. Seasoned M&A advisors will have experience and wisdom that will pay big dividends to you as a seller, quite possibly for years to come. For information about how to choose the right advisor, refer to Chapter 23 of this book.

Tax Attorney or Tax CPA

When you sell your business, you are potentially facing the single largest tax event of your life. As such, you will need to consult with an expert or experts in the field of selling businesses to determine how to minimize taxes.

Find someone (or some people) who is familiar with

1. CAPS Trust;
2. CRT or CRUT;
3. IRS Section 1202, for taxation of a C corporation, which allows for $10 million of gains to be tax-free; and
4. IRS Section 338(h)10, elections and installment sale tax law.

Each of these areas of expertise requires a specialist who is experienced enough to be able to intelligently advise you about these tax reduction strategies. This may or may not be your current CPA. The reason it may not be is he or she may not have clients selling their businesses on a regular basis.

Your trusty CPA may have served you well over the years, but he or she may not be who you need to help you minimize your taxes when you sell your business. You will need to make this determination with the help of your broker, advisor, or banker.

Additionally, you may need the following advisors to assist you through the process as well:

- Business appraiser
- Attorney who does trusts
- Lending expert or loan officer
- Raising capital expert
- ESOP expert
- Cooperative conversion expert
- Life insurance expert
- Business coach

QUESTION 4: Do I Need to Perform a Background Check on My Buyer?

While a background check would certainly be helpful, at a minimum, get on the internet and research your buyer. Take this responsibility of your own accord and be sure to leave no stone unturned. This is not a job you should delegate to your advisor or broker. Examine social media platforms and use a Google search with the prospective buyer's name and other aliases he or she may have.

Learn all you can about who you are selling to, especially if you are doing a seller carry or earnout. You can even ask for a copy of the potential buyer's credit report and credit score if you are doing a seller note. Screen your buyer's background and reputation, and always call business references and acquaintances.

QUESTION 5: Should I Delegate Some of the Selling Work to an Employee?

Selling a business may be more work than you expect. One seller commented to me that it was like having a second job. Once you start down the path of the business sale, you will find there are many tasks that only you can do. Don't turn the *pathway* of selling a business into the *rabbit hole* of selling a business.

I would recommend designating one trusted employee—or several trusted employees—to work on the sale, which will keep you on task to run the business. This may require overtime and weekend work to see the transaction across the finish line, so be prepared to compensate the trusted employee(s) assigned to the task of helping with the sale.

Remember, good books are a must! Make sure you have cleaned up the books before due diligence. Hire a CFO or controller, if necessary, to work on making your financial presentation as good as it can be. See the Appendix for a list of suggestions.

QUESTION 6: When Is the Sale of My Business Final?

The sale is final once you receive your money and all documents are executed. There will be work to do afterward, as well as a final settlement/true up in 30 to 90 days after closing, but legal ownership transfers when consideration is received and the documents are executed. Your work ends when you can walk away from your business and not be required to work there or for the buyer, which is different than the closing.

Keep in mind that the transaction can unwind at any time during the process for a myriad of reasons. One associate once commented that a deal won't close until the process has unraveled at least three times. Even though this may be a less-than-usual experience, it is not uncommon for your business sale to take a fork in the road and proceed down a different path than you may not have expected.

Accept the fact that you will work day and night to close the loopholes and finish the details of your sale. You will be driven to do your best so that the transaction closes when you want it to.

QUESTION 7: What Timeline Can I Expect When I Am Selling My Business?

Most transactions need a minimum of 30 days to close, even if the sale is 100 percent cash. When banks are involved, you should expect to add another 30 to 60 days to the process. On average, plan on 30 to 90 days to close the transaction after the LOI is signed.

Days 1–30: LOI Signed. Due Diligence
Starts. Submit Loan to Bank.

Days 60–90 Legal Phase Starts. Prepare
Legal Documents. Finalize Loan.

Days 30–60: Finalize Due Diligence.
Bank Loan Approval and Conditions.

Day 90: Finalize and
Close the Transaction.

QUESTION 8: What If the Seller Is on the Lease after Closing?

Seldom do closings occur on the exact day of the expiration of the lease. There is usually time left on the contract. When this happens, it is up to the landlord to decide if he will release the seller from his lease obligation. This release is called a lease assumption. The seller remains on the hook, and the buyer is added as an obligor for the lease since landlords aren't required to release the seller from his obligation.

The bottom line is the seller remains on the lease and is obligated under the lease until the expiration of the contract. Sellers aren't automatically released when the lease expires, and you will need to make sure you get that signed release from the landlord in the future when the lease is renewed or extended by the buyer.

In the rare circumstance that the seller is released from all liability, this is called a lease assignment.

QUESTION 9: Why Do Sellers Need to Carry a Note as Part of the Transaction?

Seller carries or earnouts are commonplace for the sale of a business because of the "money hook" or "skin in the game" aspect of the transaction. This is the common thread in which the seller wants to help the buyer succeed in the business because he or she will have a financial gain attached to that success. The seller will often assist the buyer if needed, but not always. If the seller has a vested financial interest in the success of the business, he or she will be more likely to help the buyer succeed.

For instance, we could draft a thousand-page document requiring the seller to assist in the process. But, if the seller didn't want—or wasn't motivated—to help, he or she would figure a way out of helping the buyer succeed. If the buyer succeeds, the bank has a higher likelihood of getting paid. This is why banks like seller notes. Sellers can opt not to do a seller note, but an all-cash sale is usually discounted 10 to 20 percent.

QUESTION 10: What about Training the New Owner and Noncompete Agreements?

The sale of the business will include a certain amount of free training to be provided by the seller. Typically, this can be from two weeks to 30 days. This training should be specified in terms of the number of hours and days to be provided each week. In addition, I suggest a more extended period of training on a "consulting basis" for "phone consultation." For instance, free training might be for two weeks following closing, and then the seller will provide up to 10 additional hours of phone consultation for six months following closing.

The sale will most likely also include a noncompete agreement. Check your state law, as states have different requirements about the enforceability of these agreements. Commonly, a buyer will ask the seller not to compete against him or her for two to five years in the geographic areas the business currently operates. Be prepared for this request and make sure you aren't planning on running a competing business. Ignoring a noncompete increases the risk of a seller getting sued after closing for breach of contract.

Again, good books are a must. Make sure you have cleaned up the books before due diligence. Hire a CFO or controller if necessary to work on making your financial presentation as good as it can be.

☆ BONUS TIP ☆

Be straight up and straightforward with your transactions. If there is "hair" on your transaction (see Chapter 2), disclose this up front to the buyer and figure it out early instead of waiting until later, as issues are best handled early in the sales process. Don't hide from the issues—confront them. It is okay not to focus on the negative, but don't lie to a buyer—it will hurt you and your reputation, and it could kill the transaction.

The Ugly: What They Don't Tell You

Before selling a business, few people know about the difficult parts of the transaction they will encounter. Like the good, knowing the ugly is essential as well. This chapter will cover the hard topics of which you should be aware:

- Win-Win Is Best
- Selling Your Business Is a Lot of Work
- The Transaction May Unwind Two to Three Times Before You Close
- Uncle Sam Is Your Silent Partner
- Selling a Business Is Highly Emotional, Like Selling One of Your Children
- You May Not Get Paid on Your Seller Note
- You Will Have to Face Problems Head-On

Win-Win Is Best

Selling a business is best when it is a win-win transaction for the seller and the buyer. You will need to push hard to get the main things you want and let some things go that aren't important. Prioritize your wants with your advisor, who will be your biggest ally. You won't always get everything, but a good advisor will make sure you get the most important things. Treat the sale like a marriage, not a divorce. If you treat the sale of your business like a divorce, with attorneys jockeying for every advantage they can get, it won't end well.

Selling Your Business Is a Lot of Work

When you sell your business, it will take a lot of time and effort on your part, even with help from advisors. Expect to work late hours and even some weekends to cross the finish line. Although it will be hard, it will be worth it in the end.

The Transaction May Unwind Two to Three Times Before You Close

I have painfully learned this lesson over the years. You must keep your cool and not lose your composure when things seem to unwind. The transaction may feel like it has ended and all the work was done in vain before it suddenly comes back to life. The most compelling factor for getting across the finish line is having a motivated seller working with an eager buyer, both of whom are willing to figure out solutions to the problems as they arise. Obstacles will appear; you have to work through them.

Ironically, while writing this chapter, I had an issue with an engineering firm I'm selling. The seller called because his principal office manager just quit. We were three weeks from closing, and he was worried that it would kill the transaction and scare the buyer away. I immediately notified the buyer. We set up a meeting and figured it out. These things happen all the time, but you will get through it.

Uncle Sam Is Your Silent Partner

After all your hard work, blood, sweat, tears, and years of toil, Uncle Sam will show up and demand his share. This is the starkest reality of them all. There is good news, though: There are tax-saving strategies that can work, depending on your situation.

Selling a Business Is Highly Emotional, Like Selling One of Your Children

Selling a business, which is most likely the single largest financial transaction of your life, will be an emotional roller coaster ride as you maneuver the sales process. All sellers experience this. It is normal. Therefore, it is vital to have advisors who can remove the emotion and inject logic and experience into the situation.

You May Not Get Paid on Your Seller Note

We take every precaution we can and secure the seller note with a UCC filing, yet sometimes the buyers still fail to pay the seller for the seller note receivable. This occurrence usually happens when the business isn't successful after closing, or the buyer feels jilted in some way by the seller and seeks to get even.

You Will Have to Face Problems Head-On

When I was in the mortgage business, occasionally, a loan officer would sell a client an interest rate for which the client wasn't qualified. The loan officer would disregard the fact that the interest rate wasn't feasible until the day of closing. When the client was at the closing table, the loan officer would point out that he or she couldn't get the interest rate the customer wanted. The loan officer would then sell the customer on a new rate. Sometimes this tactic worked, and the people would go ahead and sign for the loan. But every time this happened, the people left angry. It wasn't a good way to encourage repeat business!

It's human nature to put off doing things that are hard or uncomfortable. However, if we don't address problems, they tend to grow bigger. Buyers are "big boys" and can handle issues, but they are more willing to swallow these problems if they are disclosed to them earlier rather than later in the sales process. What buyers don't handle well is being deceived. They often move on to the next acquisition, leaving you behind.

I was in the middle of due diligence on a multimillion-dollar transaction when a member of the buyer's team thought we had lied to them about a non-arm's length company that was owned by the sellers. The buyer went temporarily ballistic, and the deal was quickly unwinding until I pointed out that we had disclosed the non-arm's length company in the beginning. I showed him the email, and he finally cooled down. I think he had been lied to before, which is why he had a strong reaction to perceived deceit. Had we hidden the fact that the seller owned a side business that was making money from the business he was selling, the transaction would not have closed. The seller would have lost millions of dollars.

I was involved in another transaction that didn't turn out as well. We were finishing due diligence when the buyer discovered that the seller was getting jobs by bribing the customers' decision makers. These payments didn't help the customers at all but lined the pockets of the corrupt employees. In some industries and countries, this is a common practice. It's not necessarily an ethical practice, but it is a common one. Instead of the seller disclosing this business practice, it was discovered by the buyer, who was, to say the least, angry! The transaction went south, and the seller's lack of disclosure cost him the sale of his business.

Always disclose anything unique to your business. This disclosure includes anything that the buyer will need to know about your business or business practices early in the process. We call these unique things about a business "hair on the deal." Most businesses have some exclusive details of which the buyer will need to be aware. Make sure you have full disclosure and complete transparency.

Having "hair on the deal" includes the following examples:

- Off-the-books cash payments
- Work performed on trade
- Oral contracts and side deals
- Related party transactions
- Key customers who are considering filing bankruptcy
- Employees who have given their notice to leave
- Operating under someone else's license
- Family members working for the business

It works like this: If you are going to jump into a hole in the ground and you can't see the bottom, you will want to know how deep it is first. If the hole is three feet deep, you will land differently than if it's only three inches. Buyers expect sellers to tell them how deep the hole is since they can't see the bottom. More often than not, buyers are okay if you disclose how deep the hole is in advance. But they aren't okay discovering how far down the hole goes by jumping in. This is how you end up in court after the sale of your business or giving some of the money back to the buyer for misrepresentations you made or failed to produce.

CHAPTER 3

4 Common Mistakes Made by Sellers

I recently had interested buyers walk away from a business because of two common mistakes made by the sellers. This chapter covers four common mistakes made by sellers that can undermine a transaction's ability to close and reduce the compensation you will receive when you sell your business.

These are the four most common mistakes made by sellers:

- Having Poor Financials
- Changing the Deal after It Is Agreed Upon
- Choosing Poor Advisors
- Not Being Realistic with Pricing

Having Poor Financials

The first mistake is NOT having good financials readily available. When you bring your business to market, it is imperative that you have your financials in order. Buyers who are ready to pull the trigger on a transaction will want to see a good set of financials. Any delay in delivering them will make the buyers nervous; they start to think that something is wrong or that the seller is hiding something.

Internally prepared financials are not going to cut it for most buyers. At the very least, you should have financials compiled by a CPA when selling your business. Reviewed or audited financials are even better. All of these should be prepared on a GAAP basis, if possible.

Buyers will steer clear of any misrepresentation of the financials, the operation, or other pertinent information. Take time to sufficiently represent the facts of your business, highlighting the main reasons a buyer will want to buy your business. If you aren't ready for the sale, don't present your business to market prematurely. Take the extra time to get your business fully prepared, and you will reap the benefits of your efforts.

Changing the Deal after It Is Agreed Upon

The second mistake sellers make is changing the deal after it is agreed upon. Once you have made a deal with the buyer, you can't change the terms. Buyers tend to be excited at first, but that excitement can quickly wane when a seller starts altering the deal. Buyers will get skittish and disappear if they don't feel that they are being treated fairly. You must be fair, stern, and honest. If not, you could end up not selling your business, missing out on the money you deserve, or worse, in court.

Choosing Poor Advisors

It's vital to hire the right advisors who are "deal guys" and know how to get the job done. CPAs are skilled and highly trained at compiling and analyzing historical information. However, they can kill your transaction if you let them become involved in the decision-making process. Do not let them ruin your deal with a lack of experience and knowledge about the sale and your intentions.

Well-meaning attorneys can also harm your transaction if you let them. One time, we were working on closing documents, and the seller's attorney had just completed an out-of-state case for his client. The case was a nightmare because the legal venue was in another state and he didn't understand the laws in that state. He kept reminding us of his recent bad experience and pushed so hard to get the legal venue changed that he nearly killed the transaction over a legal entanglement. Always consider your advisors' advice, but there may be times when you should *not* take their advice. You make the decision, accept the risk, and move on.

Not Being Realistic with Pricing

When selling your business, it is hard to take the emotion out of the transaction. Your business is your baby, and if you are selling it, you want top dollar. Getting the most money possible for your business is what your advisor is trained to do, but asking substantially more than what the market will bear is not realistic. If you put your business on the market for more than it is worth, it just makes the competition look good. I've seen time and time again where advisors will list businesses for sale at an above-market price, and then the business will sit for months and sometimes years without selling and eventually sell for what the market will bear. It's a waste of time and money. If your business won't realistically sell for what you need it to, take some time to build it before you sell it.

There are good business coaches who can help you scale your business. I recently had a business listed for sale that experienced exponential growth within one year. The seller lost his appetite for selling, and I suggested that we wait another year, build the business, and sell it for more money. We did just that, and he received 50 percent more than he would have had he sold two years earlier. He made more money, I made more money, and we were both happy. In Chapter 23: Choosing Your Advisory Team, you'll find a list of business coaches who can help you build your business to where you want it to be.

CHAPTER 4

How to Prepare for Selling a Business after or during Economic Downturns

As I'm writing this book, there are rumblings of another recession looming in the future. We have been on national lockdown due to the COVID-19 virus for nearly two months. I'm getting a lot of questions about how this will impact business owners in regard to the sale of their business.

Economic downturns present opportunities for people who are prepared and understand the impact. In this chapter, I will help you see an opportunity when other people see misfortune. This chapter answers the four main questions you will ask yourself as you consider the sale of your business with the threat of an economic downturn:

- **What Should I Know If I'm Considering the Sale of My Business before or during a Down Cycle?**
- **How Do I Protect and Recession-Proof My Business?**
- **How Has Selling a Business Changed in the Last Decade, and How Will It Change in the Next Decade?**
- **How Do I Make My Business Agile to Better Capitalize on an Economic Down Cycle?**

BONUS: **What Do I Need to Know about Selling a Business after COVID-19?**

The final segment of this chapter is devoted to what you need to know about selling a business after COVID-19, the most recent downcycle.

QUESTION 1: What Should I Know If I'm Considering the Sale of My Business before or during a Down Cycle?

During an economic down cycle, prices for businesses are generally reduced by 10 to 20 percent. This could equate to a lot less money in your pocket if you wait to sell. I would recommend that you do a self-assessment of your energy levels. How much gas do you have in your tank? Are you almost full, or is the light blinking on empty? If you are going to weather the storm of an economic down cycle—which very well may last 12 to 14 years, based on past economic cycles—you will need enough gas in your tank to accomplish this.

> Economic downturns typically cycle every 12 to 14 years.

Other important considerations are your age and retirement goals. If you are in your late 50s or early 60s and do not want to be forced to ride out another recession before you retire, you will want to seriously consider selling now. How old are you, and when do you plan to retire? Are you in your 60s looking to retire in five years? If so, a recession in four years would land right in the middle of your window to sell your business. You may not want to postpone your retirement into your 70s, riding out the storm for another 14 years before you can sell your business.

I see a lot of people who are now seriously considering selling their business because they understand how economic cycles work and don't have the energy or time to ride out another 12- to 14-year economic down cycle. You will need to carefully consider where you fit and how selling by design versus selling by disaster will help you reach your goals.

QUESTION 2: How Do I Protect and Recession-Proof My Business?

The first point I want to make is to identify and diversify now—don't pacify. A potential buyer asked a client of mine what he did to protect his sales during a recession. The seller, who had a logistics company, said that when times were good, people didn't hire him to deliver because they were able to purchase their own trucks. He used this as an opportunity to go out and find new customers. When times were bad, those former customers were looking to save money, so they sold their trucks and rehired him to make the deliveries. The point is that the seller was smart and figured out a way to turn past clients into current clients during a recession. This is like putting up stormproof plywood over the windows before a hurricane: It protects you and your business.

Your business will have vulnerabilities that can crush you during a down cycle. Identify your exposure and brainstorm ways to protect yourself during a storm. Perhaps you need to focus on lowering a high customer concentration. Or, you may have a product or service that is vulnerable to a down cycle that motivates you to expand your offerings. My stepfather once told me that the main regret he had in business was that he hadn't diversified his income enough. He was in construction his whole life and wished he had protected himself through diversification. It was sage advice from a savvy businessman.

QUESTION 3: How Has Selling a Business Changed in the Last Decade, and How Will It Change in the Next Decade?

Technology, the internet, and an unrestricted flow of information have made selling a business better than ever. In this digital age, individuals selling a business have 24-hour access to business listings and data. This has exponentially expanded the pool of potential buyers, opening the marketplace to a whole new world of domestic and international prospects.

Technology has accelerated the ability to collaborate with people across the country like never before. I recently closed a deal in Virginia with a group of advisors from Atlanta, sellers from DC, and attorneys from Denver and Philadelphia. We closed the transaction without everyone meeting in person. Technology has allowed us to utilize the top talent from across the country to sell businesses.

The future for selling businesses looks strong. As baby boomers start to retire, we are going to see more businesses up for sale over the next 10 to 15 years. With the information available online, buyers are becoming more sophisticated and better prepared to buy a business. All these factors are favorable for you as you consider selling your business.

QUESTION 4: How Do I Make My Business Agile to Better Capitalize on an Economic Down Cycle?

You aren't limited to making money on the sale of an asset because you make money when you buy the asset correctly. The sale of the asset is simply the action of monetizing the gains you have already made. As I look back on past recessions, businesses and other assets tended to be marked down, which led people to accelerate their purchases. People panic, and when they do, they think emotionally instead of logically. Higher emotion equals lower compensation. As other people are panicking, you will be buying because you will be prepared to pounce on opportunities as they come your way. Good deals exist now. Great deals will exist during the economic downturn. Follow the Boy Scout motto: Be Prepared!

So, how do you prepare now to capitalize on future opportunities? Here are the six best ways to prepare now:

1. Secure access to funds.
2. Banks are good at lending money when you don't need money. I would recommend securing lines of credit for your business and real estate and increasing credit limits on credit cards so they can be used in the future. Use your strong current financials to qualify for lines of credit instead of waiting until your financials have weakened. I have seen this many times: Business owners feel like they don't need a line of credit, so they don't get one, but then later kick themselves for not having it when they needed it. Remember, banks are good at giving you money when you don't need it and horrible at giving you money when you do. If you wait until you need the money, you either won't qualify for as much as you'd like or won't be eligible at all because your financials aren't as strong as they are now. Lock down lines of credit now even if you don't think you need them. These lines of credit are tools that you will use to access the cash you will need to capitalize

on future opportunities when they come your way during an economic downturn.

3. Stockpile cash.

4. I would also recommend boosting your savings plan and increasing your liquidity. During an economic downturn, you will need instant access to cash. Warren Buffett once said, "The best chance to deploy capital is when things are going down" (Eric Rosenbaum, CNBC, September 1, 2018). Opportunities will arise that will require you to have instant access to cash. I wouldn't put money into stocks or bonds or something that will take days to liquidate—put it into savings accounts. You will give up short-term gains to hit home runs later.

5. Convert underutilized assets to cash.

6. If you need to sell those assets during a recession, you will likely receive less money for them then and not be able to sell them fast enough to capture the opportunities you will encounter in the future. Identify and take an inventory of your assets to see which ones you are underutilizing and identify which ones to sell now. Liquidate those assets and put the cash in savings to make future purchases.

BONUS: What Do I Need to Know about Selling a Business after COVID-19?

The first thing to know is this: Don't let COVID-19 crush your dreams. Can you sell your business after COVID-19? YES! It will be somewhat different than before, but it can be done.

I started selling businesses in 2010, which was probably the worst year you could start selling business. What I've learned is that you can sell your business in the best of times and in the worst of times—you just need to be smart and approach it correctly.

Here's what you need to know:

1. If your business is failing, you can still sell it. Even though you have filed for Chapter 11, you can still sell your business. Don't just arbitrarily shut it down without talking to a selling advisor

first. You could lose a lot of money if you just shut it down.

> Eliminate earnout ceilings to make more money.

2. Businesses typically sell for less, but they still sell. During the COVID-19 pandemic, I sold two businesses and have listed another one for sale.

3. There are "bottom-feeder" buyers out there who will try to steal your business. You need to be tough and play hardball with these guys not to get slaughtered.

4. You need to *mind* your exit, not *blind* your exit, now more than ever. Finding an experienced business broker, M&A advisor, or investment banker to represent you is crucial to your success when selling during an economic down cycle.

5. The offers you receive will typically include shared downside responsibility. What this means is we usually see seller notes or earnouts for 10 to 15 percent of the purchase price. During economic downturns, we see those numbers increase to 20 to 40 percent. This means less cash in your pocket at closing and more paid overtime.

6. If you have an earnout, make sure it doesn't have a ceiling. I see buyers offer to pay a seller an earnout and want shared responsibility for downside risk, but I seldom see the earnout that also shares upside potential. This disincentivizes the seller to continue to grow beyond a certain point. It encourages the seller to put the brakes on the business at the exact moment he or she should be pushing the gas pedal. Structuring your earnout without a ceiling sets you up to potentially make more money than you would normally.

7. Buyers are still out there and willing to spend money. I probably get at least two or three buyers each week reaching out to inform me that they want to buy a business. They have not gone away—they are still looking for good businesses to buy.

CHAPTER 5

The 7 Deadly Sins of Cash-Basis Accounting

This chapter applies to transactions over $1 million. If your business is worth less than $1 million, it is still a good idea to understand these principles because your business may very well be valued over $1 million in the future. I explain the two methods of accounting and reveal three important lessons I've learned that you need to know to maximize the cash in your pocket when you sell your business.

As a business owner, you are likely familiar with cash-basis accounting, which is the most common method of financial reporting. This method works well for taxes and has probably served your business well for many years as a tool when you are concerned with cash flow and getting everyone paid since it is the simplest, least expensive, and easiest method of accounting.

But, as you know, simple and easy is not always the best. Why would you not want to use the easiest accounting method for your company? Because cash-basis accounting may cost you millions of dollars when you sell your business! This failure of proper accounting is what I call the *Deadly Sins of Cash-Basis Accounting*. There are seven of them. They are called deadly because they can kill the sale of your business.

Cash-Basis Accounting Method

Why is cash-basis accounting so popular? It allows a business owner/taxpayer to choose the year the income will be realized (manipulate income in any given year) using such mechanisms as holding checks and not depositing them, increasing inventory to be sold the next year, and prepaying expenses in one year to reduce or increase taxable income in any given year. The business owner can now "shift" income and expenses to or from one year to the next to defer or prepay taxes.

Cash-basis accounting is not only the simplest form of accounting, but it can also become a mechanism for tax planning for business owners.

GAAP-Basis Accounting Method

The GAAP (Generally Accepted Accounting Principles) method of accounting is much more sophisticated, complicated, and costly, so most small business owners resist this method until it is required by an outside party such as the IRS, a lender, a bonding company, or a vendor, or they are forced to use it by a buyer when they sell their business. This method involves accrual-basis accounting and the application of generally accepted accounting principles, not cash-basis accounting principles.

This type of accounting lessens the impact of revenue or expense manipulation by an owner and tends to normalize the numbers over time. It is also the accounting standard or method most relied upon by financial institutions, buyers, investors, and Wall Street.

Think about it this way: All publicly traded companies on the NYSE and NASDAQ are on a GAAP basis for a good reason: GAAP accounting is more reliable, normalizes the income and expenses, and is better for their purposes.

Modified-Accrual-Basis Method

This is a hybrid of the cash and GAAP method of accounting. It is the cash method of accounting with a few selected accruals on the financials, but not a full GAAP method of accounting.

Before I reveal the Seven Deadly Sins of Cash-Basis Accounting, you must know these three critical lessons as a seller:

Lesson #1

Buyers generally won't accept your cash-basis financials if your business is selling for over $1 million. This will require you to convert your cash-basis financials to GAAP financials. When you prepare to sell your business, the buyers are most likely going to require the more sophisticated method of financial reporting. This is true 100 percent of the time if working capital is included in the purchase price. Banks and investors often base lending decisions on GAAP financials, not cash-basis financials. If you don't have GAAP financials, you will have to produce them before closing the sale of your company.

One engineering firm I recently represented had accrual-basis financials showing double the EBITDA (EBITDA is an acronym for "earnings before interest taxes depreciation and amortization" that is commonly used as a metric for determining value) the cash-basis financials showed. This effectively doubled the purchase price of his business and amounted to another $4 million in company value! The owner had resisted my pleas to prepare his financials on an accrual basis for over six months. Once he saw the difference, he was happy to potentially get another $4 million in his pocket when he sold. When the owner realized the monetary gap, he changed his tune from resistant to exuberant. He had discovered that the additional effort was worth the increase in value to his company for the sale of his company.

With few exceptions, this is usually the case with GAAP financials. You will not always get double the value, but you will most likely get a higher value by taking the time to have accrual basis financials prepared for the potential buyers.

Lesson #2

Working capital is often a component of business sales of over $1 million, and cash-basis financials don't include working capital. Working capital is calculated as current assets minus current liabilities.

To be more specific, working capital is usually calculated as the sum of the following:

Current Assets

- Cash
- Accounts receivable, less allowance for doubtful accounts
- Prepaid expenses
- Deposits

- Inventory (sometimes excluded)
- Work in progress
- Costs in excess of revenue

Less: Current Liabilities

- Accounts payable and payables
- Accrued expenses
- Billings in excess of costs

Cash-basis accounting does not include enough information to calculate working capital since some of the above items aren't included on the balance sheet. These include accounts receivable, accounts payable, accruals, and work in progress. If you, as the seller, can't calculate or reasonably estimate working capital, you don't know exactly how much cash you will receive for your business at closing since the final selling price is based on a working capital target number, which changes minute by minute. The sale of your business is usually the single largest financial transaction in your life, so don't gamble on what the numbers will be.

As you can see from the example above, the working capital calculation requires GAAP-basis financials. If you have a savvy M&A advisor, he or she will help you set a working capital target at the letter of intent (LOI) stage of your business sale. This target working capital number will be calculated or estimated when you sign an LOI and will either reduce or increase the cash you receive at closing, impacting the selling price of your business, dollar for dollar.

Here is an example of how it works: Years ago, I sold a local pet store. The sales price was based on the seller having at least $200,000 of inventory at cost, which was to be included in the selling price. This inventory was, in effect, working capital. On the day of closing, when we counted inventory, if the inventory was higher, the selling price of the store increased dollar for dollar for everything above $200,000. If the inventory was lower, the selling price would be reduced dollar for dollar for the deficiency. The inventory number was set as a "target" to be part of the sale because the buyer wanted to make sure she knew how much inventory she was buying.

Theoretically, if this inventory target wasn't included in the selling price, the seller could have sold all of the inventory prior to closing and kept the cash, leaving the buyer with nothing. As we approached the closing date, the seller became worried about what his inventory would be because he didn't keep accurate count records of his stock. The pet store had so much inventory on the shelves that it could have easily been double what he estimated it to be. The buyer became nervous that the number would increase the selling price so much that she couldn't afford to buy the additional inventory. I had a concerned buyer and a worried seller, which wasn't the right way to approach the closing date of the business. Neither buyer nor seller knew how much money they were going to get or bring to the closing. Everything was up in the air.

This "guesswork" closing isn't how you, as a seller, want to approach the sale of your business. It is far better to be able to estimate where the numbers will be. If you know what your numbers are, then you are better able to negotiate and better prepared to get what you want from the buyer. Incidentally, we did work out the sale of the pet store. They had a large amount of stale inventory that we discounted and ended up being close to the $200,000 number after some negotiation of the inventory on hand.

Lesson #3

If you only have cash-basis financials, it puts you, as a seller, at a disadvantage in negotiation. As a result of not knowing how much working capital you have, you won't truly understand or be able to estimate how much money you will get when you sell your business because you won't know how much working capital you have or don't have.

If you only have cash-basis financials, you can't possibly know what to ask for when negotiating the purchase price since you don't know what you are selling or how much money you are getting at closing. You are "shooting in the dark" with financials, hoping to hit your number.

I recently had a transaction that reduced the cash that the seller received at closing by over $150,000. This was due to the working capital number being lower than he expected when we converted his financials from a cash basis to a GAAP basis.

7 Deadly Sins of Cash-Basis Accounting Identified

The following are seven "deadly" accounting concepts that are integral to GAAP accounting yet aren't part of cash-basis accounting. These seven concepts can and often do represent a lot of money to or from sellers, but they are often overlooked until it is too late.

Deadly Sin #1: Billings in Excess of Revenue/Costs in Excess of Revenue and Percentage of Completion Method

Billings in excess is a "financial accounting of 'over billing' where the actual revenues earned are less than the accounts receivable billed. This entry on a financial statement is shown as a liability to the company until the revenues are collected" ("Billings in excess of costs," BusinessDictionary, WebFinance Inc., businessdictionary.com/definition/billings-in-excess-of-costs.html). This accounting concept is, in general terms, when you have either billed for or received revenue for work in excess of the work you performed on the project.

Cost in excess of billings occurs when the billings on uncompleted contracts are less than the income earned to date. These under-billings result in increased assets. In effect, this creates an asset or a liability on the balance sheet. The corresponding entry also impacts revenue and expenses, which impacts EBITDA.

Since billings and costs directly impact EBITDA and the working capital calculation on the balance sheet, they have a direct impact on the selling price of your business. These numbers can go both ways: They can either increase the cash you get at closing or decrease it.

Deadly Sin #2: Accruals – Vacation, Interest, Bonuses, Wages, and Payroll Taxes

These numbers are often overlooked and underestimated by business owners; however, these can substantially and negatively impact cash to you as a seller at closing. Contrary to popular belief, these numbers don't increase your cash: They decrease it.

Accruals are amounts that you owe but haven't paid (consider them debts). For example, your vacation policy may allow employees who have worked for the business to earn vacation time that can be used in the future. This vacation time won't be on your cash-basis balance sheet, but it will be a deduction to the cash you get at closing.

I often see accrued wages because payroll is usually paid after the end of a month—say, on the first day of the following month. This payroll that is owed to employees for the previous month but paid in the next month becomes part of the accrual calculation. Accruals also impact EBITDA, working capital, and the current liabilities on the balance sheet.

Deadly Sin #3: WIP – Work in Process

The WIP number is used in manufacturing and is common in engineering firms. For engineering and architectural firms, this number represents the work that has been completed but hasn't been billed. For manufacturing firms, this number represents inventory that hasn't been converted to finished goods. With engineering firms, this represents work completed for projects but not yet billed. In the end, the WIP can represent a tremendous asset—typically, an increase in the amount the seller receives at closing—and directly impacts EBITDA and working capital.

Deadly Sin #4: Prepaid Expenses – Deposits, Leases, Insurance, and Licenses

These items usually represent smaller dollar amounts than the other six deadly sins. However, these can still amount to tens of thousands of dollars in the seller's favor. Prepaid expenses are for all expenses that are prepaid as of the day of closing. They impact EBITDA and working capital.

Deadly Sin #5: NOL – Net Operating Loss and Tax-Deferred Assets

I was recently working on the sale of a C corporation as a stock sale that had a large net operating loss (NOL) carryforward. This is an asset that, if identified, can be additional money to you as a seller of a C corporation with a stock sale. The NOL impacts the balance sheet only and is included in the working capital calculation, which is a part of cash at closing to the seller.

Deadly Sin #6: Capital Leases

A few years back, I was selling an equipment rental business. This company had hired a good tax accountant who helped them minimize their taxes, which is a standard business practice. For tax purposes, they were able to write off the cost of the leases in one year, which minimized their taxes. However, when we did accrual-basis financials, the leases had to be capitalized, which means they had to write off the cost of the leased equipment over five years instead of expensing it all in one year. The bottom line is that it added $400,000 to its EBITDA. This business sold at a 3.5 multiple of EBITDA, so it increased the value by a whopping $1.4 million!

Deadly Sin #7: Accounts Receivable and Accounts Payable

Accounts receivable and accounts payable are amounts that are owed by or to the business. Be careful and review how the AR and AP as of the closing date compare to the AR and AP balances at the end of the previous year. This difference between the two will impact the EBITDA. For instance, if AR is increasing, this will positively impact EBITDA. However, if the AR is lower, this will negatively impact EBITDA. You might have collected the AR early to shift income in one year, which will help cash flow for cash-basis accounting but hurt EBITDA for accrual basis accounting. AR and AP impact working capital, the balance sheet, and EBITDA.

CHAPTER 6

Important Acronyms and Buzzwords

This chapter contains a list of buzzwords and acronyms you will encounter when selling your business that are important to become familiar with.

Adjusted EBITDA (Earnings before Interest, Taxes, Depreciation, and Amortization)

This is becoming more commonly used than EBITDA due to business owners having more discretionary expenses that are eligible to be removed in the straight EBITDA calculation. The difference between EBITDA and adjusted EBITDA is discretionary expenses.

Bandwidth

This refers to the capacity of the business to grow by increasing current products or services.

Capital Expenditures (CAPEX)

CAPEX is the amount of expense a business incurs for the purchase of equipment on an annual basis.

Cash Flow

This can mean EBITDA, SDE, or cash flow.

Confidentiality Agreement (CA) or Nondisclosure Agreement (NDA)

These are two names for agreements that are signed by a buyer before the buyer is allowed to see the CIM or COM, which contains detailed information about the business being sold. These are important parts of every business sale since they bind the buyers contractually to confidentiality during the sales process.

Confidential Offering Memo (COM) or Confidential Information Memo (CIM)

These both refer to a book of detailed information about the business being sold. They are given to buyers once they sign a CA or NDA. Buyers use them to learn more about the business being sold because they have detailed information about the financial and operational aspects of the business. Other names for these are "the book" or "pitch deck."

Discretionary Expenses

These are expenses that an owner takes to reduce his or her tax burden but aren't necessarily going to be expenses for the new owner. These include a one-time lawsuit, automobile expenses for the owner, health insurance for the owner, perks, etc.

Earnings before Interest, Taxes, Depreciation, and Amortization (EBITDA)

EBITDA is the most common metric used to derive value. Value is often derived as a multiple of EBITDA.

Financial Buyer

This type of buyer is more concerned with the financial metrics and performance of the business than with how the business can be utilized along with his or her other businesses to create added value. Typically, a financial buyer won't see as much value in the business and will offer a lower price for it than a strategic buyer. Due diligence will typically be focused more heavily on the financials since they are the most important thing to a financial buyer.

Gross Profit

Sales, revenue, or earnings minus cost of goods sold equals gross profit.

Letter of Intent (LOI)

An LOI is a document that outlines an agreement between two or more parties to purchase a business. It has both binding and nonbinding aspects to it.

Indication of Interest (IOI)

An IOI expresses a buyer's intent to purchase a business. It is usually less binding than an LOI.

Earnings

This has multiple meanings and can mean gross revenue/sale/income, net income, cash flow, EBITDA, or SDE. Because of this, it is essential to define it in the LOI.

Earnout

This refers to a way for a seller to be paid in the future, after closing, based on a specified metric. The common metrics used for the earnout are gross revenue/sale/income, net income, cash flow, EBITDA, or SDE. For the seller, it is preferential to base the earnout payments on a net number versus a gross number because there is less room for the buyer to manipulate the numbers at his or her discretion.

Leveraged Buyout (LBO)

An LBO is when a bank or other financing is used to buy a business.

Post-Closing Sure Up or True Up

Since the sale of businesses has many moving parts and there are transactions in process at the time of closing, a final settlement or sure up is necessary for a buyer and seller to settle up and pay amounts due to either party. This is usually done 30 to 45 days after closing. Every precaution is taken to cover everything up to closing. Invariably, there will be money collected or discovered after closing that is either owed to the buyer or owed to the seller. I tell the sellers I represent to keep track of these and bring the list to the final settlement. The buyers will do the same.

Profit

Profit is used synonymously with gross profit, net income, cash flow, or EBITDA.

Runway

This refers to the capacity of the business to grow by offering new products or services.

Scale

This is the capacity of a business to grow, usually exponentially.

Seller's Discretionary Earnings (SDE)

SDE is an estimate of the total financial benefit a full-time owner-operator would derive from the business on an annual basis. The main difference between this and EBITDA is owner wages (read more at vikingmergers.com/blog/2015/sellers-discretionary-earnings-explained/).

Seller Note

This is similar to a second mortgage on a house, except it is a note which is carried by the seller for the sale of a business, usually secured by the business itself. The buyer owes the seller money for the seller note, traditionally paid over three to five years. For instance, a common structure for a $1 million sale would be for the seller to carry a note for $100,000, the bank to finance $750,000, and the buyer to bring in cash of $150,000. The seller would be paid his or her $100,000 over time like the bank, only it is a separate note receivable owned by the seller.

Strategic Buyer

This type of buyer is motivated by how he or she can leverage the business along with his or her current assets—whether they be another business, product, service, or opportunity—to create value by combining the new business he or she acquires with another asset. In this instance, if you do the math, it would be like the equation $2 + 2 = 5$. Combining the business with the other asset creates greater value than the two have independently. Strategic buyers usually don't care as much about the financials as they do the potential, and due diligence tends to be simpler and easier when a strategic buyer is buying the business.

Working Capital

This sometimes, but not always, includes the following: cash, accounts receivable, deposits, inventory, and all current assets minus accounts payable, accrued liabilities, and current portion of long-term debt and all current liabilities. The accounting definition is simply current assets less current liabilities. Each buyer has an opinion of what working capital includes, so it is important to agree upon the working capital calculation when the LOI is executed.

THE PROCESS OF SELLING A BUSINESS

CHAPTER 7

14 Steps to Selling Your Business

This chapter identifies and explains each of the 14 steps to selling a business.

STEP 1: Considering a Sale

Wondering about the process, price, market timing, and what to do next is the first step to selling your business. This step may take years to get you to where you want to sell. This is normal.

STEP 2: Contacting and Choosing a Selling Advisor

Contacting and contracting with a good selling advisor is paramount to the sale of your business. A sales advisor is not your attorney or accountant—he or she is a business broker (transactions under $1 million), M&A advisor (transactions between $1 million and $30 million), or investment banker (transactions over $30 million). You can sell on your own, and some people do, but I would recommend hiring a selling advisor for the single biggest financial transaction of your life. You will initially choose your selling advisor, then add other members of your advisory team when the time is right. The selling advisor is the quarterback of the team.

Choosing the right advisor and advisory team is such an important step in the process that I've devoted a whole chapter to the topic. For information about choosing advisors, see Chapter 23: Choosing Your Advisory Team.

STEP 3: Valuation Assessment and Timing

You will talk to or meet with an advisor to discuss and discover the estimated market value of your business. This process generally requires either a formal valuation by an independent outside third party or an informal valuation performed by the advisor. Be prepared to present at least three years of financials and tax returns.

Once you determine the estimated market value of your business, you will need to decide if this selling price will get you enough money to make the sale worth it. Remember to consult with your tax advisor at this stage to determine the worst case, net cash in your pocket. If the selling price is lower than what you want, then your advisor should strategize with you and draft a roadmap containing specific benchmarks you need to meet in order to hit the selling price you want to attain.

There are times that I will work with sellers for several years to get them where they want to be before we take their business to market. Sometimes it is only a matter of finishing out the year to prove the projected numbers. Your advisor will help you plan the best time to take your business to market. I have a word of caution: Don't get in a hurry unless you absolutely need to sell right away.

After determining market value and deciding if the estimated market value will get you enough money to sell, you and your advisor will work together to determine a marketing strategy. This may or may not include giving buyers a selling price for your business. You may want to let prospective buyers determine the selling price. I've sold businesses both ways but prefer to give buyers a selling price (or selling price range) for the business.

These are the main reasons for disclosing a selling price:

1. It is common practice to provide a selling price on businesses offered for less than $20 million.
2. In my experience, buyers often offer well below what we are asking, and it wastes everyone's time.
3. Buyers don't pay more than the market price unless there is a good reason. We leave certain things open that we can negotiate

in the seller's favor, like working capital and inventory, if the price is lower than what we want.

4. It turns buyers away. They want to know the price before they spend time looking at it, so they don't waste their time.

For businesses priced over $20 million, a bidding process is a common practice because they are in high demand and receive multiple offers. In a bidding process, you won't disclose asking price.

STEP 4: Prelisting Preparation

You and your advisor will work together in this stage to prepare your business to be listed for sale. This is an important step in selling by design, not by disaster. You will need to make sure your advisor understands your business financials, model, customers, and revenue mix, as well as the products and services you provide. He or she will give you a list of questions to answer.

Your advisor will prepare a book, pitch deck, and confidential offering memorandum (or offering memorandum) for your business. This will be the write-up that will be given to buyers after they have signed a confidentiality agreement. Make sure you read all the marketing material your advisor sends out to ensure its accuracy.

STEP 5: Listing

Once everything is prepared, your advisor will formally list the business for sale confidentially. This usually includes listing on internet sites, sending emails to his or her pool of buyers, and sending a teaser to prospective buyers.

At this point, you will do phone calls and site tours with prospective buyers. Review Chapter 10: How to Prepare for a Site Tour with a Potential Buyer before conducting any tours. It usually takes five tours before receiving an offer. I like to schedule site tours with multiple buyers back to back. It is good for buyers to learn they aren't the only ones looking. These meetings are usually 60 to 90 minutes long and will give the buyer the opportunity to ask more specific questions. If there is a bid process in place, this stage will involve bringing multiple buyers to a presentation and interview.

Site tours can be on-site or off-site and during or after business hours, depending on the sensitivity of the employees. I suggest off-site or after hours, if possible. The last thing you want to do is have your employees wondering who is poking around. One thing I suggest is giving each buyer a little something when they visit, if possible and practical. If you make a product, give them one. If you have a marketing promotional shirt, give them one. This may seem like a small gesture, but it works magic with buyers. It keeps you in their mind. Remember, potential buyers may be looking at dozens of businesses, and this helps yours to stand out. I had a recent seller give a buyer a pocketknife with his logo on it, and the buyer was excited by this gesture. It was small, simple, and effective. This tactic works!

STEP 6: Offering to Purchase

This is the fun part. Ideally, your advisor should get multiple offers that you can choose from. The offer generally comes in the form of an LOI for transactions over $1 million and an offer to purchase for transactions under $1 million. Written offers are necessary. Your advisor will present the offer to you. At this stage, since you may be giving up the right to continue to market the business, you will want to vet the buyer. It is customary to get a statement of net worth from the buyer or proof of funds or a bank letter of approval.

LOIs typically do not have numeric examples of calculations for earnouts, profit sharing, and working capital, so I like to have the buyer give numeric examples of the important calculations in the LOI. This requirement has saved my sellers and me a lot of headaches. Make sure you understand everything in the LOI. If you have questions, this is the time to ask them.

STEP 7: Acceptance, Rejection, or Counteroffer

You will either accept, reject, or make a counteroffer. Unless the offer isn't worth considering, I would suggest making a counteroffer. I do not burn bridges. As much as I'd like to grab the gas can and torch a bridge sometimes, I won't do that. Ever. You just never know when you will be working with a person again.

STEP 8: Mutual Acceptance

When the buyer and seller agree to all terms and conditions of the sale, the LOI is signed, and you are "under contract." Remember that either party can back out at any time.

STEP 9: Due Diligence

Due diligence is the inspection phase of the transaction. This is where you open up and show the buyer everything except for proprietary information. Review Chapter 3: 4 Common Mistakes Made by Sellers for a list of what not to show to buyers and what is okay to show buyers. Due diligence may be done on-site or remotely. The buyer will usually have a team of advisors with whom he or she will be working.

STEP 10: Contingency Removal

Buyers remove all contingencies of the agreement. This formal removal of contingencies is usually done with transactions under $1 million but may be done on any business sale. It involves the buyer signing a contingency removal to release earnest money to the seller. After the contingency removal, the earnest money is nonrefundable under certain conditions. Earnest money isn't common in the sale of businesses but can be a part of any transaction, if need be.

STEP 11: Legal Document Preparation

The beginning of this phase is what I look for during due diligence as a sign that we are moving toward closing. Buyers will tell you they are having their attorney start the preparation of legal documents. This means they are okay spending money on the legal aspect of the transaction because they feel comfortable with the information they have examined so far. I look at this as a very good sign we are going to close the transaction. However, it doesn't mean due diligence is over—it just means due diligence is nearing an end. This step overlaps due diligence to expedite the closing. The sentiment of the transaction moves from "Are we going to do this?" to "How do we get this closed?"

The legal preparation phase of the transaction involves the preparation of between 20 and 250 pages of documents. This can be laborious and frustrating. Luckily, good attorneys relieve us of that burden. You will just want to get the transaction completed so you can move on. This is where everyone can suffer from "deal fatigue." Emotions run high, and tempers can flare. Use your advisor as a sounding board and an outside third party to maneuver the "sticky points" of the transaction.

STEP 12: Closing

Closing involves the legal execution of the documents, wiring money, and receiving money. In some cases, the signature pages are signed before closing, and the closing itself is merely the attorneys approving the amendments and releasing the signature pages you have already signed. Buyer and seller don't need to be together for the closing. It is often handled remotely. It is *not* held at an escrow or title company unless the bank or sale of real estate requires it.

The bank doesn't always fund the transaction the same day as closing. It may take up to five business days for funding. The transaction can, in rare instances, not fund. Make sure you have the money in your account before handing your business over to the buyer and releasing proprietary information.

STEP 13: Final Settlement and True Up

Final settlement and true up is the phase where the numbers are finalized and any amounts due to or from the seller are paid. This is done 30 to 90 days after closing.

STEP 14: Transitional Training

To ensure a smooth and successful transition of ownership, it is customary that the seller continues to work with the buyer for a period of time following the closing date. The transitional training period varies depending upon the size and complexity of the business.

CHAPTER 8

Launching Your Business for Sale, Not *Listing* Your Business for Sale

When it comes to selling your business, my suggestion is you should never *list* your business for sale. Instead, you need to *launch* it.

I'm not a fan of prematurely listing your business for sale before you and your business are ready. That's why the first two steps to launching your business for sale involve preparation and the third step is execution. I'm going to walk you through these steps and the processes involved so you will know what to expect and how to hire an advisor who can help your sale to take off.

STEP 1: Advance Preparation

When considering the sale of your business, it is never too early to speak to a sales advisor to plan for the sale. Meet with your advisor as soon as you begin considering the sale of your business to map out your strategy for selling. There have been times when I have worked with people for over three years to plan an exit. You don't want to go to market prematurely unless you are forced to. The better you plan, the better prepared you will be to get the most money for your business and have a successful sale.

Along with meeting with your chosen advisor, you will need to do a self-evaluation of your finances, accounting, and operation. To help you with this, I've provided checklists to address common weaknesses I've encountered.

Finances and Accounting Presale Checklist

You will need to identify weaknesses in the numbers and in your reporting with the help of your CPA. Having accurate financials is imperative for getting the most money for your business. Here is a checklist of common accounting weaknesses in small businesses:

- ☐ **Income Reports** – Is all your cash being reported? If not, deposit all of it and report it as income. I've represented businesses where the owners were literally putting 25 percent of their sales in their pocket and not reporting it. Had the owners spoken to me beforehand, I would have had them deposit the money, pay the taxes, and report it as income to get him a much larger selling price.

- ☐ **Accounts Receivable** – Clean up, write off, and collect on any accounts that are over 90 days old.

- ☐ **Inventory** – Write off, donate to charity, or sell stale or unsaleable inventory.

- ☐ **Reporting Frequency** – I would suggest having monthly financials prepared for your business, including a balance sheet and profit and loss statement.

- ☐ **Compiled Financials** – I would suggest getting annual compiled financials prepared by an outside CPA firm for three years.

- ☐ **Trade Work** – If you are doing work on trade, you will need to report this in the financials. Consult with your CPA about how to record these expenses and income.

- ☐ **Held Checks** – Do not hold checks or prepay expenses at the end of the year to shift income to another year.

- ☐ **Monthly Billing** – Make sure you are current on your monthly billing and stay current. If there is a need for your employees to turn in hours worked or timesheets for you to bill, look at ways to accelerate the time the work is completed and the time you bill for the service.

The Business Operation Presale Checklist

Just like with your finances and accounting, your operation needs to be evaluated to prepare for the sale of your business. Here is a checklist of common problems to look for:

- ☐ **Verbal Contracts** – If there are verbal contracts with customers, employees, vendors, manufacturing facilities, or anyone you do business with, you will want to convert them to written contracts.
- ☐ **Length of Contracts** – If you are planning to sell your business, having long-term contacts with customers beyond the sale date is optimal. If you have contracts for expenses, it is preferable to have shorter terms for these contracts unless you are getting a price discount. Look at your contracts and assess what is best moving forward as you consider executing or renewing contracts.
- ☐ **Minority Owners** – You will want to contact the other owners to make sure they agree with the sale or are at least aware of it.
- ☐ **Personal Guarantees** – Since personal guarantees will need to be removed, you will want to investigate early on how to get these removed prior to listing your business for sale.
- ☐ **Employees** – If you have employees that need to be reprimanded or fired, it is best to do that prior to listing your business for sale.
- ☐ **Lease** – If you are planning to sell your business and have a lease that is coming due, you will want to assess the best terms for you and what a buyer would want. See Chapter 13: Golden Nuggets of Wisdom for Unique Transactions and Businesses for guidance about leases.
- ☐ **Vendors and Customers** – You will want to do everything you can to maintain good relationships with vendors and customers in preparation for the sale.
- ☐ **Management** – If changes in management need to be made, make them. If you have people who will need to be groomed to step up in your place, get to work doing that task. Remember, the business needs to run better in your absence than your presence!

STEP 2: Final Preparation

This step is where you and your advisor will compile the documents to send to buyers. It is important to have everything ready to send before moving on to Step 3. You will want to ride the wave of enthusiasm with buyers and get them the information they need as quickly as possible. I've experienced lackluster responses from seller advisors before, and they undermine the value of the business with the buyer pool. Here are the steps involved in this preparation:

- Spend between one and two weeks with your advisor preparing a 20- to 30-page offering memorandum to be sent to qualified buyers who have signed an NDA. It is imperative that your advisors have the information correct before it is presented to buyers—the reason being your best buyer may be one of the first buyers. You don't want to blow through the best buyers with a mediocre offering memorandum. I like to ride the wave of enthusiasm when they get excited about the business and give them what they are looking for right away. This helps keep the momentum going.
- You will need to answer a detailed questionnaire provided by your advisor so he or she can better understand your business. This includes questions he or she has compiled in the past while working with buyers. Experienced advisors will have a good list of questions that they know buyers will want to have answered.
- Your advisor will prepare, and you will review and approve everything before sharing it with buyers.
- Determine the asking price with your advisor and refer to the valuation you should have previously completed. You will work together to determine the asking price of your business based on market and internal factors, as well as your timeline for selling.
- Your advisor will prepare a teaser marketing piece to send to buyers who have not signed an NDA. This will happen after completing the offering memorandum and in preparation for the next step.

I have three advisors that I recommend for helping you prepare for the sale of your business if your time horizon for selling is more than nine months. These professionals aren't M&A advisors, but they are experts in the field of preparing your business for a sale, each with his own specialty. See their credentials in Chapter 23: Choosing Your Advisory Team.

- Garrett Gunderson, Wealth Factory, wealthfactory.com
- Brandon Allen, New Work Revolution, newworkrevolution.com
- David Leis, Avantt Consulting, avanttconsulting.com

STEP 3: Execution

You will not have to do much work in this step. However, your advisor will be working diligently to give maximum exposure to the worldwide pool of potential buyers. These are the steps involved in the execution of launching your business:

- Your advisor will send the teaser to his or her pool of qualified buyers within 24 hours. These buyers have worked with your advisor before, or they have approached him or her about buying a business. The potential buyers include, but are not limited to, private equity groups, venture capital groups, investment bankers, high net-worth individuals, other M&A advisors, business brokers, and business owners looking for an excellent opportunity.
- Within the first week of listing, your advisor will use the teaser to conduct a blast email campaign, phone calls, and texting campaign as an outreach to potential buyers.
- Your advisor will upload the teaser to the largest, most-trafficked listing services and websites (over 70) around the country to attract multiple strategic buyers within the first weeks of listing.
- Your advisor will contact, screen, and work with potential buyers and buyer agents. After they have signed the NDA, your advisor will send them the offering memorandum. The offering memorandum will save you time by answering many of the buyers' initial questions.
- Some marketing campaigns involve a bid process where the asking price is not included in the offering memorandum. This is more common for transactions over $10 million but can be used in any sales transaction.

CHAPTER 9

What You Need to Know about Due Diligence Requests

D ue diligence usually takes between 30 and 45 days to complete but may take longer if bank financing is involved. Being aware of what to expect before you enter into this phase of the transaction will help you make a better representation to buyers. I've provided a Due Diligence Checklist in the Appendix for your reference so you can see the items that buyers commonly request. This list is not comprehensive, as each transaction lends itself to a unique set of circumstances, but it provides you with a reasonable foundation.

Buyers address the following eight items while performing due diligence:

1. Business Name, Owners, Status, and Licenses

2. Assets

3. Liabilities and Leases

4. Financial Documents

5. Real Estate Lease and Location

6. Operations, Customers, Business Practices, and Employees

7. Legal Issues

8. Insurance

1. Business Name, Owners, Status, and Licenses

Buyers will verify the legal status of the business, which will include the business name, address, legal status within the state you are doing business, and contact numbers of the business through the Department of Commerce. If you do business in multiple states, they will want a list of these licenses so they can make sure they are current. If the business owners, principals, or key employees are required to have professional licenses, they will check the status of their licenses with the state. Buyers will contact the regulatory agencies that govern the business to get a rating of the business and ask questions about transferring licenses. They will also check if the principals have criminal records.

Assume buyers will look online at reviews on Google, Glassdoor, Facebook, the Better Business Bureau, your website, and elsewhere on the internet. An internet search for published articles about the company and its owners or principals will also be performed. Corporations, partnerships, and sole proprietorships have public information available from the state as well. They will find out if your company is active and current in filing its yearly documents as required by law. Checks will be done with the issuing licensing agency to verify that licenses and permits are valid and up to date.

2. Assets

Buyers will request to receive a complete list of assets included in the purchase. These assets include FF&E (furniture, fixtures, and equipment), inventory, and real estate. Make sure the assets have clear titles, the equipment has been inspected, and everything is in working order. If a fleet of vehicles is purchased, maintenance records are necessary to confirm the quality of care. You will also want to identify any assets not included in the sale of the business. This includes personal and business vehicles that you plan on keeping after the sale. Ownership of real estate assets can be verified in the county's assessor's office, and motor vehicles with the Department of Motor Vehicles. Transfer of ownership will happen at closing.

3. Liabilities and Leases

Buyers will ask for a list of liabilities that will be paid by you at closing and a list of liabilities that will be assumed at closing. This will include copies of the real estate leases as well. The landlord(s) and other entities that you have commitments to may require written permission to transfer the liability to the new owner. These third-party consents and approvals will need to be obtained prior to closing. The buyer and his or her attorney will review the leases and assumed liabilities. You will need to know what these leases are, how much the monthly obligations are, the rules and restrictions of the leases and liabilities, expiration dates, delinquent payments, and past-due amounts owed.

4. Financial Documents

The buyer and his or her team of advisors will review three to five years of financial history to understand how the company performs and to prove the accuracy of the numbers. They will look at both tax returns and internally prepared financials. A CPA firm is often hired to do a mini-audit and write their opinion based on their findings called a Quality of Earnings Report. Your financials will be scrutinized. They will study the profit and loss statements, balance sheets, accounts receivable, accounts payable, tax returns, vendor invoices, bank statements, payroll and sales files, employee files, equipment maintenance documents, and other vital data. Sometimes, they do their work at your place of business. If they do, be prepared to have a conference room available for their team of advisors. Remember that CPAs are good at auditing records and preparing tax returns, so buyers will use them to check for accuracy and consistency.

5. Real Estate Lease and Location

At the end of due diligence, the buyers will want to take care of the lease assignment. At this point, you will notify the landlord that you are selling. Wait until the very end of the process to notify the landlord of the sale to avoid creating unnecessary alarms.

If your location is important, the lease will be a crucial part of the negotiation. Buyers will examine potential threats to the business from competitors, especially those in the vicinity. They may go to the city's planning department to find out if there will be future road or building construction that may decrease foot and vehicle traffic, or if a large competitor is planning to build in the area. If you own the building, buyers may or may not want to purchase the real estate. If they do not initially purchase the real estate, they usually negotiate an option to purchase in the future.

6. Operations, Customers, Business Practices, and Employees

The buyer will do a full examination to understand your operation, customers, and employees. They will want to know how you obtain and retain customers and employees and learn the functions and responsibilities of your employees. Buyers will also want to learn how you generate revenue, how it is accounted for, and your marketing techniques.

7. Legal Issues

County courts have records on judgments and liens against the business owners and tax liens. Buyers will check those. If unexpected liens pop up, they will need to be paid at closing, or proof will need to be provided that the liens have been paid and debts satisfied. State records have the UCC (Uniform Commercial Code) filings that contain any liens against the business that need to be paid at closing.

There are many records that can be accessed for free online or through agencies and information providers for a fee. Specific licenses and contracts may need to be transferred with the sale of your business. You will need to identify these and determine how they will be transferred. In some instances, the licenses and contracts will only transfer if the entity is purchased. This will force a stock/entity purchase instead of an asset purchase.

8. Insurance

A buyer will examine your insurance coverages to assess his or her future insurance needs. You will need to talk to your insurance agent ahead of time if the buyer wants to continue to use the same company.

The buyer will need to make sure he or she has insurance in place on the day of closing. Buyers will sometimes hire insurance experts to give them guidance about the types of liability coverage they need. The specialists provide insight into things like malpractice, umbrella coverage, errors and omissions, general business insurance, property and casualty coverage, limits, etc.

As a seller, you want the buyer to know that you are cooperating. The due diligence process can become frustrating, particularly when you receive repeated requests for mounds of different documents. Be patient with the process and your buyers. Use your broker, M&A advisor, or banker if the demands become tedious.

CHAPTER 10

How to Prepare for a Site Tour with a Potential Buyer

Sellers often ask questions about what to do and how to handle a meeting with a potential buyer. This chapter contains critical insight for you to prepare to meet the buyer for the first time.

Site Preparation

While this may seem obvious, site preparation is essential to selling your business. The saying that "first impressions are lasting impressions" is true. You only have one chance to make a first impression, so do everything you can to make it memorable.

Assess the location where you will be meeting, taking steps to ensure that it is tidy and clean. It's a good idea to provide some extra housekeeping the day before the meeting. If you own the property, spruce up the outside of the building and clean up any trash or graffiti that may be in view. If you're meeting in a conference room, make sure it is presentable. Remove the clutter from desks around the office and organize the files. Paying attention to these details will help create a strong first impression with the buyer.

Questions That Buyers Ask

- What are your plans after closing?
- Why do you want to sell?
- What keeps you up at night? What are your most significant worries?
- Who are your key employees? What are their intentions about staying?

- What are some questions I should be asking you about your business?
- From where is the revenue derived?
- Describe your customer concentration.
- What makes your business unique?
- Who is the competition? How do you compare?
- What is your pricing model for your products or services?
- How long is left on the lease?

How to Dress

On the day of the tour, you will want to dress as you usually do when you go to work. Make sure your clothes are clean and presentable if your business is more casual. If your business requires business attire, then wear your best suit, shirt, and tie. As an advisor, I will prep the buyer as to how he/she should dress to match the occasion. I usually encourage buyers to dress more casual to not attract attention to themselves.

Believe it or not, buyers also ask me how they should dress. We try to match the buyer with the seller so both parties feel comfortable.

What to Say

- Be natural and express the passion you have for the business.
- Highlight the good things about your business.
- Disclose any information or "hair on the deal" that he or she will need to know as a buyer.
- Listen to the buyer and do not talk over him or her. The conversation should be natural and not rushed.
- Don't over-answer the questions. What I mean by that is this: If they ask what time it is, don't tell them how to make a clock!

What Not to Say

- Don't point out all the flaws of your business. Highlight the positive. Don't elaborate on the reasons you are selling the business or why you no longer care for the business. I've had to counsel many sellers to avoid pontificating over unfortunate events that may have occurred years ago. Don't wear negative experiences like a badge of honor—the buyer doesn't care about it. Be simple and direct. There is beauty in brevity.

- DO NOT LIE. Buyers will sniff out a lie and move on to the next business in the blink of an eye. If you do not feel comfortable telling the seller a potentially bad piece of information, then defer to your advisor.
- Answer their questions, but don't answer the questions they don't ask. Sometimes sellers will go on and on with an answer to a question that buyers never asked. Once you have answered your buyer's question, stop and let him or her ask another. Don't feel required to fill the silent gaps in the conversation.
- Do not talk about the terms of the deal without your advisor. You hired an advisor to represent you, so let your advisor do his or her job. You will be far better off and get more money for your business by using your advisor to handle the negotiation.

What to Do If You Get a Question You Don't Want to Answer

Sometimes, we get a buyer who asks a question that the seller doesn't want to answer. For instance, "What is the name of your top customer?" As a seller, you don't have to divulge proprietary information at this point. If this happens, defer to your advisor. You could say something like "You are going to have to talk to my advisor about that." Or, you may turn to your advisor and ask, "What do you think about that?" It's also okay to not answer the question immediately and tell them you will get back to them with an answer.

Website and Social Media

Take a minute before the tour to go to your website and make sure it is working correctly and everything is updated. Buyers will do their due diligence before the tour, which includes visiting your site. You'll also want to inspect your businesses' social media accounts, including Facebook, LinkedIn, and Instagram. Look at each of these, update the information (if needed), and remove anything that may not be appropriate.

I recently had a deal that did not go through because one party's website was not working. For weeks, the site showed that it was under construction, and the other party did not want to deal with it. The buyer thought it was a bad sign that reflected a seller who didn't take care of his business.

Keep the Meeting to an Hour

You want the buyer to see your business and have an opportunity to meet you, but you do not want to make it an all-day meeting. You have work to do, and the buyer needs to assimilate the information he or she receives. If you give the buyer too much information, it is the same as giving a person a drink from a fire hydrant: They can't handle it.

Confidentiality

I prep my buyers ahead of time as to the confidential nature of the tour. Buyers should know that they are not to ask questions in front of the staff. Hold the meeting in a private place without interruptions. If this is not possible, schedule the meeting someplace outside the business.

Questions to Ask Buyers

You will want to get a sense and feel of the buyers you work with to not waste time. I like to start with general questions about the buyer's background, education, and experience. Learn about the buyer's business culture/business philosophy if he or she currently owns a business. Will it meld into yours? Can you see this buyer as a fit for your organization? You will need to ask questions about the buyer's experience, creditworthiness, cash position, philosophy about employees and customers, and fitness (i.e., will he or she be a fit for your business culture).

Here is a good "boilerplate" list of questions to ask buyers:

1. What is your experience running a business?
2. Have you ever run a business like this before?
3. How do you plan to fund the purchase?
   - Are you planning to use bank financing?
   - If so, can you provide a preapproval letter?
   - The bank will require at least 15 percent down. Is that a problem?
4. Will you have partners? If so, can we meet them and understand that relationship?

5. How is your credit? (It is good to know this because you may need to do a seller note.)
6. What are your plans for the employees? Will pay rates change?
7. Will the benefits change?
8. Will you relocate and run the business (if you are out of state)?
9. What are your plans with current management?
10. Why are you interested in this type of business?
11. How will the transition work?
12. What will be my (the seller's) role after closing?
13. Will you be engaged in the day-to-day operation after closing?

Always follow your gut. What I mean by that is this: No matter how good the dollars look, listen to your feelings. If it doesn't feel right, don't do it. Find another buyer.

CHAPTER 11

Types of Buyers You Will Encounter While Selling Your Business

As a seller of a business, it is essential to know the types of buyers you will encounter in the sales process. Successfully selling a business requires the help of an advisor who "knows the ropes" and has dealt with every kind of buyer. The three basic types of buyers are financial, strategic, and partner. This chapter will also cover how a cash buyer differs from an LBO buyer. Powerful insight will be presented as to what buyers are thinking when they're considering your business.

The 3 Basic Types

Financial

Financial buyers like to base their buying decisions on the numbers. It is all about the numbers, multiples, and financials (both historical and projected). They tend to be industry agnostic because it doesn't matter what type of business it is; it only matters what numbers the business can produce. I would call them the bean-counter people.

Bankers and business appraisers usually are enlisted to provide comfort and figures for the transaction. It's all about how the numbers look, particularly if the EBITDA and SDE (seller's discretionary earnings) numbers indicate potential growth for the business.

Financial buyers tend to like businesses that have had robust and steady growth over the past three years versus a recent jump in revenue. You will feel like you are having a full audit of your financials because they'll want to see evidence of stability and reliability. Financial buyers like facts, numbers, and logic.

Strategic

Strategic buyers tend to be less about the numbers and more about the opportunity provided by the acquisition. Don't get me wrong: They care about numbers, but in the back of their mind, they care more about how this business will fit into their existing business plans.

For example, imagine you had five acres of real estate surrounded by property that was owned by a developer. If this developer was motivated to develop all of the land, including yours, your five acres would most likely be worth much more because it was the final piece of a bigger puzzle. As a result, he would pay a premium for your five acres.

Strategic buyers tend to pay more because the business is worth more to them as it fits into their overall strategic plans. When working with a financial buyer, you will want to figure out the buyer's whole plan and emphasize how your business will fit into that plan. Strategic buyers tend to scrutinize the financials less than financial buyers, so due diligence is usually faster and easier.

Partner

A partner could be either strategic or financial. Partners generally want the seller to hold equity post-close. Partners typically acquire 20 to 90 percent of a business and work with the seller to grow the business post-close. Partners can provide financial support, management oversight, and guidance that the seller of a business lacks.

How a Cash Buyer Differs from an LBO Buyer

Cash Buyers

A cash transaction is a possibility with financial, strategic, and partner buyers. However, there are essential considerations to be aware of when dealing with a cash transaction versus a financed transaction. Buyers who have cash typically want a discount off the purchase price. If these buyers are buying the business using their life savings, they are going to be very careful and will run away from the transaction if they sense something they don't like. You could say they tend to be flighty. If you have a buyer like this, I would accept backup offers in case the buyers walk away. It's always easier to work with buyers who aren't investing their life savings to buy the business.

LBO Buyers

Buyers who are buying the business with the help of the bank will be more focused on getting the loan than performing extensive due diligence. The basis of the transaction will be about the bank being able to get the loan. Make sure your buyer is qualified and has an approval letter from the bank, but understand that the bank approval letter doesn't guarantee a sure thing. Banks can pull the plug on the transaction at any time, sometimes right before closing. Working with banks can be frustrating. They can delay the process for weeks and sometimes months, but, in the end, they do fund loans. SBA will fund loans up to $5 million. Other types of bank loans need to be used to fund loan amounts over $5 million.

Important Fact: Buyers Don't Always Know What They Want

Buying a business can be a frustrating, painstaking process that can sometimes take years to complete. Buyers often research hundreds of businesses to find the right one, which takes time and money. The truth is buyers want to spend their money and need to be pointed to favorable circumstances.

One thing I've considered over the years is specializing in selling one type of business. Every time I get close to specialization, I am reminded that buyers don't know exactly what they want. Sure, you get the dentists who only want dental practices and engineers who only want engineering firms, but these types of buyers represent a small segment of the market.

Buyers in the broader market segment think they know the type of business they want, but what they really want is value and opportunity (runway). They want to look at a lot of different businesses and decide which one they like. You could say they prefer a buffet to a menu.

Years ago, I was in the process of closing on the sale of an industrial bakery. The bakery sold to a membership-only warehouse club and had a good business model. On the day of closing, the buyer did an inspection of the equipment to ensure that it was working correctly. There was a big industrial machine that the seller was supposed to fix prior to closing. When the buyer inspected the device, he discovered the seller lied about repairing it properly. The buyer lost trust in the seller, and the sale unwound. The business did not sell that day. The buyer was upset, angry, and felt like he had been deceived.

We went back to my office, where he asked to see what other businesses I had for sale. When I pulled out my portfolio, he was immediately enamored with a custom motorcycle dealership. We went to see the owners, and he fell in love with the business and bought it.

As I look back on this transaction, I can't think of two businesses that are more different than a bakery and a motorcycle dealership. It proved to me that when motivated buyers want to buy a business, they're open to a variety of opportunities. They are hungry to make a purchase, and it doesn't matter what type of business it is.

CHAPTER 12

You Have a Letter of Intent. Now What?

Once a letter of intent (LOI) is signed, you are considered "under contract." This means that the seller and buyer both commit to taking the next steps in anticipation of closing. The LOI usually has both binding and nonbinding provisions. One essential item to note is that transactions can and do fall out after an LOI is signed. Nothing is guaranteed at this point. Let's look at the four steps buyer and seller will take after an LOI is signed: due diligence, legal document preparation and negotiation, closing, and shore up or final settlement.

Due Diligence

I often refer to this stage of the transaction as the "courtship stage." The seller has chosen a prospective buyer to buy his or her business, and it is time for the buyer to scrutinize the business finances and operations. There is a phrase from Japan that best describes this phase, the translation of which is "Open the kimono." This means that the seller will freely share all of the information—except for sensitive information that could jeopardize employee or customer relationships—with the buyer. The buyer will do a financial and operational audit by hiring people to test and prove the numbers the seller is required to provide. He or she will inspect the business for misrepresentations, fraud, potential problems, opportunities, and so forth.

Both parties will be analyzing the other to decide if this is indeed what each wants to do. During this inspection phase, the seller can also request information about the buyer. The seller will vet the buyer during this process as well to determine if he or she will be a fit for the business, customers, and employees. Keep in mind that the nonbinding sections of the LOI allow for either party to back out of the transaction at any time during due diligence. Due diligence is commonly done at the seller's business but can also be done off-site. It is usually up to the buyer to decide how to manage due diligence.

This phase also includes getting bank approval for the loan if the business is to be financed, which is commonly referred to as a leveraged buyout (LBO). Expect the due diligence process to take two to four weeks.

Legal Document Preparation and Negotiation

This phase, which generally takes two to three weeks, is not usually started until the buyer has determined—and is confident—that he or she is going to buy the business. The buyer's focus moves from "Are we going to buy this business?" to "How do we get this across the finish line to closing?"

The buyer's attorney prepares the necessary closing documents, and the seller's attorney will review them and make comments. There is a bit of negotiation that is done at this point to fine-tune the documents and make the transaction fair to both parties. If the attorneys push each other too hard, the buyers and sellers may need to step in and take control to get the deal done.

Closing

This is the day when all of the parties fully execute the necessary documents to legally transfer ownership of the assets of the business or the company itself to the buyer.

Actual signatures or written authorization is required to release signature documents previously signed. It can be done in person or by email or fax. The sale of a business, if real estate isn't involved, can be done in an office rather than a title or escrow company. In many cases, the buyer and seller will sign the signature pages of the contracts a few days ahead of time. Then the documents will all be held in escrow with the attorneys and later released with written notice so there isn't an actual signing the day of closing. These preparations help to make the closing day less hectic.

Shore Up or Final Settlement

The sale of businesses has many moving parts, including transactions in process at the time of closing. That means a final settlement or shore up is necessary for a buyer and seller to settle up and pay amounts due to either party. These are usually done 30 to 45 days after closing.

Every precaution is taken to cover everything up to closing. Invariably, there will be money collected or discovered after closing that is either owed to the buyer or owed to the seller. I tell the sellers I represent to keep track of these and bring the list to the final settlement. The buyers will do the same. If a holdback was done, it will usually be released within a few days of the final settlement.

CHAPTER 13

Golden Nuggets of Wisdom for Unique Transactions and Businesses

This chapter contains the many tidbits of wisdom I've learned over the years that pertain to unique businesses or industries. Each "golden nugget" is unique and may or may not apply to you, but if it does, you will need to be aware of it. I call them nuggets because knowing this information is like having money in your pocket when you sell.

CAPEX

If your business requires a large amount of CAPEX, this will be an adjustment downward on EBITDA. This means that your EBITDA will be reduced for annual CAPEX, thus reducing the value of your business.

C Corporations—Double Taxation

We cover this topic in earlier chapters. When a C corporation is sold as an asset sale, there is double taxation to the seller.

Credit Card Processing

When you sell your business as an asset sale, the credit card processing accounts and hardware need to be replaced with the buyer's credit card processing accounts and hardware. This may take a few days after closing, and the buyer will use your accounts until he or she can get new ones set up in his or her name.

Customer Deposits

If you have received customer deposits for work in process, these will need to be negotiated in a manner that is fair to both buyer and seller based on the percentage of work completed.

Dealerships

With automobile, boat, RV, motorcycle, or power sports dealerships, the flooring interest is not deducted from the EBITDA calculation like it is with other businesses. This is unique to businesses that have a flooring line of credit used to finance inventory. The reason for this is because interest is an ongoing expense, so it can't be deducted to increase the EBITDA number.

There are four things to keep in mind when selling dealerships:

1. The buyer will need to qualify as a new dealer, meeting dealership requirements of net worth, credit, and owner credentials.
2. The flooring lines will need to be transferred to the buyer, and he or she will have to qualify for those.
3. The state will have dealer licensing requirements, and the buyer will need to meet those.
4. The lease is important, and a lease with long-term options for renewal is preferential. You don't necessarily want a long-term lease, but having a short-term lease with options for renewal with long-term options is best if you are considering a sale.

Dentists

When dental offices are valued, buyers consider three things:

1. The average age of the equipment
2. Cash pay billings versus insurance company billings
3. The fact that, unlike other dental offices, orthodontic practices usually include and are valued with the patient receivables included in the asking price

Engineers

There are several unique aspects to the sale of engineering firms, which include the following:

Transitions of the Management Team

You will need to negotiate the employment contracts of the sellers carefully. It is important to align expectations and fully disclose how you, as the seller, want to transition out of the business. This should include a plan for replacing you.

Working Capital, WIP, Costs in Excess of Billings

Engineering firms will have a certain amount of these, which may not be accounted for with cash-basis financials. This will most likely be part of the selling price and will need to be calculated, preferably well before closing. Switching to accrual-basis financials is highly recommended and preferential for an engineering firm.

Stock Sale

The sale of engineering firms is usually on a stock-sale basis due to insurance regulations that require "trailing insurance" to be paid by the seller when he or she sells on an asset-sale basis.

Financing Agreements and Contracts

If you have financings, providers, service agreements, or contracts that will be assigned or assumed by the buyer, you will need to make sure the personal guarantees associated with these agreements are released to release you from any future obligations under the contracts. You will want a release of all personal guarantees as of the date of closing.

Franchises

When selling a franchise, there are three things you need to be aware of:

1. The buyer will need to be approved as a franchisee.
2. The buyer will need to do training as a new franchisee.
3. The transfer fees will need to be paid. Negotiate up front who pays for those.

Insurance

If you have a business where your insurance rates are low due to your lack of accident history (trucking, logistics, transportation), you may have an argument for a stock sale because the new owner will start over and have higher insurance rates.

Inventory

If your sale includes inventory, you will need to determine how to handle the sale of slow-moving, obsolete, and unwanted stock. Here are some tried-and-true methods I've used successfully for selling inventory and equipment:

- Discount the inventory based on preset criteria, such as old or stale inventory that won't sell.
- Exclude this inventory from the sale and sell the excluded inventory on consignment. When these items are sold, the seller gets paid.
- Exclude the unwanted inventory and give it to the seller.
- Create a table using criteria about the age and past sales of the inventory. Then apply a discount to each type of inventory on which you agree.
- The buyer buys all the inventory, and the seller gives a credit to the buyer for the stale or old inventory.

Don't just give it away. Even if you get paid a little, it does have some value. These methods can also be used for other assets that the buyer does not want, like accounts receivable or equipment.

Leases

If you are doing a stock sale, you will need to notify the landlord. This is called a Consent to Change of Ownership, which will need to be signed before closing.

Licenses

State laws may require a license to own or operate the business. For example, when selling a construction company, it is vital to make sure the buyer has adequate licensing in place. If a general contractor's license is required to own or operate the business, the buyer will need to have a contractor's license personally, have an employee who has the license, or utilize the license of the seller.

In some instances, the license can only be transferred after the sale. I once sold a restaurant and bar that had a liquor license that was required to operate the business. The problem we had was the state required the license and would only transfer the license after the sale. We resolved this by negotiating an agreement with the buyer that allowed him to continue to use the license of the seller until he could obtain a new license. The seller had to oversee the business and meet the state-mandated requirements of the license until the buyer was able to transfer the license into the buyer's name.

The following is a list of some of the businesses and professions that require a seller to be mindful of the licensing requirements. If you are selling one of these types of businesses, you will need to deal with the licenses. While this list is not all-inclusive, it represents the industries I've encountered in my career:

- Construction companies (general contractor's license)
- Engineers (PE)
- Accountants (CPA)
- Dentists (DMD, DDS)
- Doctors
- Chiropractors
- Veterinarians
- Automobile dealers
- Real estate brokerages
- Liquor licenses
- Specialized licenses for any industry

Each state has its own licensing requirements, so you will need to check with the state(s) in which your business operates to ensure that you meet the requirements for licensure.

Master Service Agreements (MSA)

Oil-field related companies have contracts with customers called Master Service Agreements (MSA). These contracts are written approvals to do business with and bill customers. Without an MSA, you can't do work at an oil-field site. More importantly, you can't get paid for doing the work. Depending on the competitive landscape, these MSAs can be almost impossible to obtain. They become extremely valuable when selling an oil-field business. Buyers and their attorneys should take every precaution to ensure the transferability of the MSAs.

Medicare and Medicaid Billing

When selling medical-related companies that bill through Medicare or Medicaid, you need to make sure that the proper consents and licenses are given before the closing. The buyer will need to be able to bill customers after closing. The same holds for provider and service agreements.

Retail

Location matters in retail businesses, making the lease term very important to the buyer. Make sure you disclose the terms of the lease to the buyer early in the sales process and make any necessary negotiations regarding the lease well before closing.

Sales Tax

In Utah, when a business is sold, there is a form called TC-69C. When filed, this form notifies the State Tax Commission of a change of ownership and responsibility for paying the taxes. When you sell your business, if you pay sales tax, you will need to notify the states in which you do business of the sale. Each state will have its way of handling this, but make sure you take care of it. I learned this the hard way recently when I applied for a state withholding account and discovered that I was still the owner of record for a business I had sold over 15 years before. Luckily, we were beyond the statute of limitations, and I didn't have to pay a tax bill that was owed by the people who bought my business!

If you pay sales tax, the buyer will often get a certification that the tax has been paid and is current. I once had a sale fall through because of this. It was a bridal shop, and the seller didn't think she had to pay sales tax. The buyer found a significant tax lien the day of closing, and the business did not sell. Keep your taxes current, and you won't have any problems.

SBA

When the buyer is doing a loan with the SBA, you will want to be aware of these six points:

- The SBA says they will loan up to $5 million, but that is rare. They will go higher, but only with a LOT of collateral. They usually top out at $4 million.
- There are two sets of underwriting guidelines to follow: one for the local bank and one for the SBA. Local banks typically have guidelines that are stricter than the SBA, and not all local banks have the same guidelines. Some banks like business loans with intangible assets, and some banks don't like those types of loans. Consult with your advisor about which banks are best for your business.
- Your lease will need to have options to cover at least 10 years or the term of the SBA loan—whichever is less.
- If you do a seller note, you may be required to put the loan payments made to you on standby until the SBA loan is paid in full. This means the buyer won't start paying you until the SBA loan is paid off. There are ways around this that still satisfy the bank. Talk to your advisor about this requirement.
- You will need a seller note. This rule isn't written, but it is common. Banks will only approve loans with few exceptions unless the seller has some skin in the game, meaning the sellers need to carry a note—usually 10 percent of the selling price.
- Sellers can't be involved for more than a year in the operation of the business.
- The SBA may require the seller not to be paid for a seller note for a time until the SBA loan is paid in full or a specified time period has lapsed.

CHAPTER 14

Guidelines for a Successful Transition

I have seen a lot of transitions over the years, some good and some bad. This section will cover the process of the transition of the new owner. I will share information to help you have a successful transition, including the following:

- How to Announce the Sale
- A Handoff, Not a Sellout
- How to Tell Employees You Have Sold
- What to Tell Clients
- The Best Timing for Announcing the Sale

How to Announce the Sale

The notice of the sale is usually done at a mandatory meeting with everyone present. You will want the new owner there as well to make the introduction. The announcement will likely be a shock to the employees, so you will need to have the meeting on a day of the week that does not allow them to think or read too much into it.

Which day of the week is best to tell everyone? I prefer Tuesdays or Wednesdays. Mondays are too hectic, and Fridays give employees too much time to go home and think and correspond with each other, letting negative feelings and rumors abound. Tuesdays or Wednesdays are best because employees will get the announcement and be back to work the next day.

You want to make the announcement and address their questions and concerns immediately. Afterward, the best thing you can do is get back to work and show the employees that it is "business as usual."

I like to have food at the meeting as well. It allows everyone to sit down and eat something good, talk, and listen.

A Handoff, Not a Sellout

The sale is a handoff, not a sellout. It is a marriage, not a divorce. Treat it as such. As the seller, you are responsible for giving a good handoff. No one else can do it, and your people are counting on you.

Selling a business is about more than money, and your employees should understand that. Tell them your story, how you came to the decision to sell, and why you wanted to sell. Let them know you see this sale as a good thing for the company, employees, and customers. Tell them why you picked this buyer. Compliment the buyer in front of them; you wanted a good replacement, and you feel like this buyer is that person.

How to Tell Employees You Have Sold

My experience has been that employees need to be put at ease about three things: money, security, and duty. They need to know that their pay isn't going to change (unless it is), their jobs are secure, their duties will be the same, and their workload won't change unless it is to make things better.

Key employees and the leaders need to be told before anyone else about the sale. They will get their feelings hurt if you do not pull them aside and tell them personally. If you get the key employees and leaders on board with the sale, they will help sell it to the other employees. Once leaders are engaged, the others will likely follow.

What to Tell Clients

Some sellers choose not to tell clients they have sold, and you will have to decide what is best for your situation. If you decide to tell clients or customers, key clients are like key employees: They will need to be told in person or with a phone call.

Pick your top clients and tell each of them in person. You may take them to lunch individually as well. They will want to know that the products or services aren't changing and that prices will remain the same. You cannot guarantee this, but you can tell them that you see this sale as a good thing for them and for the company moving forward. Offer a cell number so they can call you if they have any concerns or questions and you can inform the buyer of any problems.

You can also take the buyer with you and make a personal introduction as well to help solidify the relationship. You will also want to give them the buyer's contact information so they can call him or her. Keep the buyer in the loop regarding problems or concerns.

When it comes to announcing the sale to the public at large, you have two choices: a quiet release and a full-on, large-scale announcement. With a quiet sale, there is not any press release at all. You choose who knows about the sale and who does not; only a few key people are aware of the sale. With a press release, the whole world can potentially know about the sale.

The Best Timing for Announcing the Sale

There are three schools of thought when it comes to timing the announcement of the sale to the employees: immediate, slowly over time, and delayed.

1. **Immediate.** With this scenario, everyone is told right up front about the sale of the business. There is no equivocating. It is done and announced, and everyone moves forward.
2. **Slowly over time.** With this scenario, the seller and buyer work more as partners and slowly tell the employees that the business has been sold in steps over time. They usually say they are partners at first; over time, they announce that the new partner has bought the business.
3. **Delayed.** This scenario is part of a quiet sale. There are times when the buyer and seller do not want anyone to know that the business has been sold. The seller usually continues to work at the business

just like he or she did before, and everything continues as if the sale did not go through. Sometimes, the employees are never told or, at the very least, are told long after the sale is completed.

SALES STRUCTURE TYPES AND COMPENSATION

CHAPTER 15

3 Sales Structure Types

When considering the sale of your business, it's essential to know which sales structure best fits your needs. Negotiating the right structure can have a significant impact on the amount of cash you, the seller, receive after paying taxes. I don't care as much about selling price as I do about cash in your pocket.

As a general rule, people will tell you to do a stock sale because stock sales are subject to capital gains, which are taxed at lower rates; however, before you push hard for this type of sale, consult with your tax advisor because it may cost you more money than an asset sale.

This chapter covers the three sales structure types. You may very well have heard of the first two—an "asset sale" and a "stock sale," which are common sales structure types—but I will also introduce you to a hybrid of those two that few people know about called a Section 338(h)10 Election Structure. Understanding these three different ways to structure the sale of your business is important because the consequences of each offer three very different legal and tax outcomes.

> Three sales types, three *vastly* different outcomes.

Asset Sale

This is the most common way to sell a business. An asset sale is simply the sale of the tangible and intangible business assets to a buyer. It usually includes all of the business assets, unless specifically excluded.

New Entity Is Created and Old Business Name Transfers

With an asset sale, the buyer creates a new entity that is used to purchase the business assets. The assets are placed into this new company. The name of the company being bought is transferred to the buyer's new company. The buyer then operates under a Doing Business As (DBA) certificate with the state in which he or she is operating. This allows the name of the old company to remain and transfer with the sale of the business.

The Old Company Is Closed

After the assets are sold, you are left with a "shell company" that is a legal entity with no assets. The shell company is typically left open for a few months after closing until it isn't needed anymore. It can be left open if you desire, but it seldom is. When the entity is closed down and the assets are sold, it mitigates any future liability against the business entity. It does not, however, mitigate the risk for future litigation based on historical events. The buyers only have risk associated with the new entity moving forward with an asset sale.

These actions provide a "clean break" for taxes and potential litigation to the seller and buyer. You will file a final tax return for your company after it is closed down.

Allocating Purchase Price to the Assets

Since you are selling multiple assets, the purchase agreement will need to include an allocation of the purchase price to the assets being purchased. The purchase price is allocated based on the negotiated value of the assets and later reported to the IRS on IRS Form 4797, on IRS Form 8594, and as ordinary income.

Negotiating and agreeing to this allocation of assets is important since the numbers for the seller and buyer need to agree when they are reported to the IRS. Here is an example of an allocation table from a purchase agreement and how the allocation may work, as negotiated, based on a $6.5 million purchase price:

Asset Allocation – Example of $6.5 Million Purchase Price

In regard to the purchase and sale of the assets of SELLING COMPANY NAME dated below located at ADDRESS HERE, the purchase price shall be allocated in the following manner:

Class I Assets – Cash	250,000
Class II Assets – Bonds and Publicly Traded Stock	–
Class III Assets – Accounts Receivable	1,375,000
Class IV Assets – Inventory	675,000
Class V Assets – Furniture Fixtures Equipment Buildings, Vehicles	450,000
Class VI Assets – Goodwill, Noncompete Agreement	3,750,000
Total = Purchase Price	**6,500,000**

_____   _____

Seller Signature   Date

_____   _____

Buyer Signature   Date

For a complete description of the asset classes, see the Instructions for Form 8594 available at irs.gov/pub/irs-pdf/i8594.pdf.

The negotiated and agreed-upon allocation of assets is reported on IRS Form 8594. The form is designed to notify the IRS of how the assets will be allocated in the future for the buyer's tax returns. The buyer and seller must negotiate and agree upon the asset allocation prior to closing since the numbers will be reported to the IRS on Form 8594. If the allocation swings too heavily one way, giving the seller a greater tax advantage than the buyer or vice versa, then one of them will lose money. This negotiation of the allocation of the assets is part of every business sale transaction.

Depreciating the Assets – Restart

The assets you sell to the buyer are stepped up in basis for the buyer, meaning the buyer can begin depreciating them based on the purchase price of the assets as specified in the asset allocation schedule. The easiest way to understand it is to think of selling one asset—let's say it is a truck: When your business sells a truck to another person, say for $30 thousand, that person can start depreciating that truck all over again. It doesn't matter what you bought the truck for. The same is true if you buy a used truck—you can depreciate it based on *your* purchase price, but not the original purchase price.

> Asset sales are the most common type of sales structure.

I've had a lot of questions over the years pertaining to why the buyer gets to depreciate the business assets a second time. The buyer's ability to depreciate the business assets purchased is highly advantageous and a huge tax benefit to the buyer. This depreciation (and amortization of goodwill) offsets future taxable income, which is why most transactions are structured as asset sales.

For example, for a $5 million sale of depreciable and amortizable assets, the future depreciation and amortization expense can be used to offset $5 million of taxable income over one to 15 years.

Negotiating the Asset Allocation

When negotiating the amounts to allocate to each asset class, it is important to consider what will be the most beneficial to each party. If one scenario is better for the buyer, it is generally worse for you as the seller. Here is why: If you allocate a higher purchase price value to equipment, then you will pay more tax as ordinary income. (Equipment has a recapture of depreciation that is taxed as ordinary income. Ask your CPA.) It is better for you to place a higher value on the goodwill since that is taxed as a capital gain.

> Allocate as much to goodwill as you can since it is better for taxes.

Buyers prefer that a higher value be allocated to the equipment versus goodwill because they can depreciate equipment at an accelerated pace in the future, either 100 percent for the first year (under Section 179 of the IRS code) or five to seven years. Buyers still get to amortize goodwill, but it is amortized over 15 years.

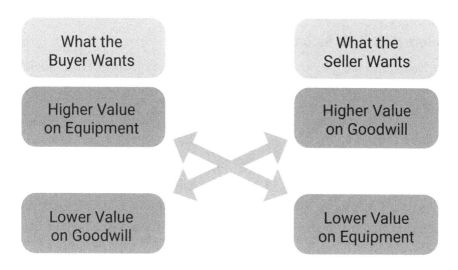

Past Depreciation Gets Recaptured as Ordinary Income to You

When assets are sold by a seller, this creates a taxable event. The past depreciation expense is recaptured as ordinary income and taxed at those higher rates. There is a capital gain portion of the sale as well that is taxed at the lower capital gain rates. These assets you are selling may have a basis, which will reduce your gains. It is important that you consult with your CPA when considering the sale of your business. He or she will be able to make the complex calculations you will need to assess your final tax burden. For tax reduction strategies, refer to Chapter 22 of this book.

Employees, Vendors, and Customers

An asset sale also requires the buyer to rehire the employees immediately after closing since he or she will have a new EIN and company. Vendors and customers will continue to write checks using the same company name, but they may have to be set up anew in the accounting system as well. If customers customarily transfer money for payment, these customers will need to be notified of the new bank account.

Bank Account

Since the company will be new, a new bank account is established with a new EIN. Pay particular attention to automatic drafts, automatic deposits, and automatic payments that were paid to/from or deposited into the old bank account. These will need to be set up in the new account.

Nature of Seller's Income from the Sale

The seller will have both capital gain and ordinary income from the sale of the assets. The sale of cash and inventory will produce no gain or loss on the sale because they are sold at their tax basis.

Lease

The lease is either assumed (the buyer takes full responsibility and the seller is relieved of his or her lease obligation) or assigned. In an assignment, the rights of the lease are assigned to the assignee (buyer). The seller remains liable to the landlord should the buyer default in an assignment.

Assignment – No Release

Assumption – Full Release

C-Corporation Double Tax

This seemingly small statement has a huge impact on C corporations. Here is how it works: With a C corporation, when you sell the assets, the gains are recognized within the C corporation. They don't pass through like they do with a subchapter S corporation or partnership. This means that if you own a C corporation and do an asset sale without employing tax reduction strategies, you will pay a tax on the gains within the corporation and another tax when you take the money out of the C corporation as a dividend. You are literally taxed twice on the sale of the assets. This makes stock sales much more attractive for C corporations.

C corporations can, under certain circumstances, make a subchapter S election for tax purposes prior to closing. Consult your CPA to see if this is an option that works for you.

Documentation

Legal contracts are typically between 30 and 250 pages long, including the schedules.

Representations and Warranties

The seller will be required to make certain representations and warranties about the assets and business. Standard representations and warranties are common with asset sales.

Unique IRS Forms to File

The unique forms to file with the IRS are Form 4797, and ordinary income will be reported as it normally is on your tax returns.

Stock, Entity, or Membership Interest Sale

The second-most common type of sales structure is what is commonly referred to as a stock sale. This structure involves the sale of the shares of stock (for a corporation) or membership/partnership interest (for an LLC or partnership). The entity itself is sold and remains intact after closing. Preservation of an existing entity fulfills the purpose and needs of the buyer and seller.

With a stock sale, the potential for future litigation based on past events necessarily creates additional reps and warranties in the legal documents to be made by the seller. This structure is usually done out of necessity rather than by choice because of the loss of future depreciation and potential legal issues moving forward. If you think of this transaction like buying all the stock of a publicly held corporation, it will help.

Here are a few examples of necessity:

- Contracts in the business name with customers won't transfer with the sale of the assets.
- Leases in the business name that provide favorable terms won't transfer with the sale of the assets.
- Master service agreements in place will be lost if the entity isn't sold.
- Other outside factors necessitate a stock purchase for the buyer.
- The buyer is a publicly held company that requires an entity purchase.

Depreciation of the Assets

When the stock is sold, the assets continue to be depreciated as they were prior to the sale. One important consideration that often gets overlooked is what I call the long game. Buyers who are considering selling the business in the future should consider a stock or entity purchase. Buyers can easily be so focused on the details that they miss the big picture, which is this: If the buyer depreciates the assets, the buyer recaptures the depreciation expense as ordinary income when he or she sells the business as an asset sale. If the buyer buys the stock or entity, the buyer has a higher basis in the stock when he or she sells in the future as a stock or entity sale, which means the buyer pays less tax when he or she sells the business in the future.

Allocating Purchase Price to the Assets

This is not applicable since no allocation of the assets is required. There are rare instances where the buyer will specify an amount for the noncompete agreement only.

The Entity and Business Name

These remain with the sale of the company.

Employees, Vendors, and Customers

The employees won't have to be rehired, and the sale is seamless for the vendors and customers.

Bank Account

The bank account remains the same unless the buyer wants to open a new one.

Nature of Seller's Income from the Sale

The seller's income is 100 percent capital gains from the sale of his or her stock, membership, or partnership interest.

Lease

If the lease is in the name of the company being purchased, then the only requirement is the consent of the landlord, which is typically a requirement in the lease. If there are personal guarantees by the owners, these will need to be released at closing or at the end of the lease term, if possible. If the lease is in the name of the seller, then the lease will be treated like an asset sale.

C-Corporation Double Tax

Not applicable.

Legal

The entity exists in perpetuity after the sale.

Seller Risk

Selling the business transfers the risk of future liability for future transactions to the buyer, but it doesn't mitigate the risk for future litigation based on historical transactions.

Risk to Buyer

The buyer only has risk associated with the new entity moving forward. With that being said, the buyer will be the new agent of record in the state he or she is doing business in. If the business is ever sued in the future for past actions and the plaintiff prevails, it could impact the business negatively, particularly if the seller doesn't meet his or her obligation. There is a certain amount of risk to the buyer in a stock sale that is nonexistent in an asset sale.

For this reason, the representations and warranties of the seller are more extensive with a stock sale than with an asset sale. Sometimes, the contract will specify a holdback amount of money to be placed in escrow for a specified time period to cover any future known or unknown liability that may exist.

Documentation

The contracts are generally shorter overall for a stock purchase, but representations and warranties of the seller are more extensive. Legal contracts are typically between 30 and 150 pages long, including the schedules.

Representations and Warranties

The seller will be required to make certain representations and warranties about the assets and business. These are extensive.

Unique IRS Forms to File

Schedule D for the sale of the stock will need to be filed.

Section 338(h)(10) Election Structure

This type of structure is a hybrid structure combining elements of both asset sales and stock sales. It is not as common as an asset sale or stock sale; in fact, your advisor may not even be aware of it. This structure is one in which the sale is treated as a stock sale for legal purposes and an asset sale for tax purposes.

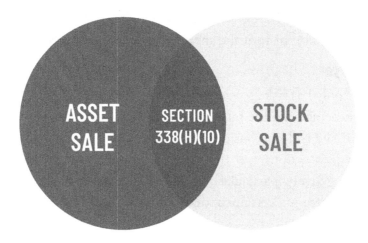

Why would you need this structure? The answer is simple: It is designed to allow sellers to sell their business and allows the IRS to still get paid as though it is an asset sale. This usually benefits the buyer, but the seller benefits because without it, the seller wouldn't be able to sell, or the business would likely sell for a much lower price.

Years ago, I was selling a logistics company in Colorado. The state of Colorado had just legalized the sale of marijuana with the mandate that the marijuana had to be grown locally indoors in order to sell it locally. Local marijuana growers started gobbling up lease space in warehouses to grow marijuana. The impact on commercial real estate rates in Colorado was fast and dramatic. Warehouse lease rates quadrupled overnight.

The company I was selling happened to have long-term leases in the name of the corporation with extremely low rates and long-term options for renewal. If we did a stock sale, the buyer would inherit the low lease rates as part of the sale. If we did an asset sale, the buyer would not be able to take advantage of the low lease rates. The buyer wanted the lower lease rates, or he wouldn't buy the business. Due to an astute tax advisor (Russell Lombardy, II, Esquire, of Monarch Wealth Attorneys), this is when I learned about a Section 338(h)(10) election. We did a Section 338(h)(10) transaction, which satisfied both buyer and seller. Without this type of structure, the business wouldn't have sold.

> Section 338 is a hybrid structure and not widely known.

Allocating Purchase Price to the Assets and Where Reported

The purchase agreement will need to include an asset allocation schedule just like an asset sale structure. This structure requires both buyer and seller to sign off on how the assets will be allocated to make the Section 338(h)(10) election. You will jointly file an IRS Form 8023—no later than the 15th day of the ninth month, beginning after the month of the closing—to make the election and a Form 8883 to allocate the purchase price among the acquired assets.

Also, if you forget to file, Rev. Proc 2003-33 grants an automatic extension of 12 months from the time that an inadvertent failure to file on time is discovered.

If the allocation swings too heavily one way, giving the seller a greater tax advantage than the buyer or vice versa, then one of them will lose money. This negotiation of the allocation of the assets is part of every business sale transaction doing a Section 338(h)(10) election.

The Entity and Business Name

The same as a stock sale structure, these remain with the company when sold.

Depreciation of Assets

The assets are depreciated identical to an asset sale structure.

Employees, Vendors, and Customers

The same as a stock sale structure, the employees won't have to be rehired, and there is no change to the vendors and customers.

Bank Account

The same as a stock sale structure, the bank account remains the same unless the buyer wants to open a new one.

Nature of Seller's Income from the Sale

The same as an asset sale structure.

Buyer's Tax Ramifications

The same as an asset sale structure.

Lease

The same as a stock sale structure. If the lease is in the name of the company being purchased, then the only requirement is that consent of the landlord needs to be obtained, which is typically a requirement in the lease. If there are personal guarantees by the owners, these will need to be released. If the lease is in the name of the seller, then the lease will be treated like an asset sale.

C-Corporation Double Tax

Same as a stock sale.

Legal

The same as a stock sale structure, the entity exists in perpetuity after the sale.

Seller Risk

The same as a stock sale structure, selling the business transfers the risk of future liability for future transactions to the buyer, but it doesn't mitigate the risk for future litigation based on historical transactions.

Risk to Buyer

The same as a stock sale structure, the buyer only has risk associated with the new entity moving forward. With that being said, the buyer will be the new agent of record in the state in which he or she is doing business. If the business is ever sued for past actions and the plaintiff prevails, it could impact the business negatively, particularly if the seller doesn't meet his or her obligation. There is a certain amount of risk to the buyer in a stock sale that is nonexistent in an asset sale.

For this reason, the representations and warranties of the seller are more extensive with a stock sale than with an asset sale. Sometimes, the contract will specify a holdback amount of money to be placed in escrow for a specified period of time to cover any future known or unknown liability that may exist.

Documentation

The contracts are smaller, but representations and warranties of the seller are more extensive. Legal contracts are typically between 30 and 150 pages long, including the schedules. Additional wording is typically added to the contract, oftentimes specifying the buyer's intention to make the election.

Representations and Warranties

The seller will be required to make certain representations and warranties about the assets and business. These are extensive.

Eligibility

The buyer and seller must both be corporations with limits. Check with your tax advisor about availability.

Unique IRS Forms to File

Form 8023, the election form, and Form 8883 (the form to disclose the allocation of the assets) will need to be filed, in addition to Form 4797 for the sale of business assets. The ordinary income will be handled like it normally is.

QUICK GUIDE
Asset/Stock/Entity/Section 338h10 Sale Comparative Analysis

DESCRIPTION	ASSET SALE	STOCK/ENTITY SALE	SECTION 338(H) (10)
The Entity	Assets are sold, and the old entity is closed. Name is transferred to the buyer.	Legal entity is transferred. Buyer owns the old company.	Legal entity is transferred. Buyer owns the old company.
Business Name	*Sold (DBA)*	*No change*	*No change*
Depreciation of Assets	Depreciation starts over with stepped-up basis.	Depreciation continues.	Depreciation starts over with stepped-up basis.
Asset Allocation	*New one per PA*	*Not applicable*	*New one per PA*
Employees	*Rehired by new entity*	*No change*	*No change*
Vendors	*Set up with new entity*	*No change*	*No change*
Customers	*Set up with new entity*	*No change*	*No change*
Bank Account	*New one set up*	*Can keep old or new*	*Can keep old or new*
Nature of Seller's Income from the Sale	Sale is part ordinary income and part capital gains. Some assets have zero gains.	*All capital gains*	Sale is part ordinary income and part capital gains. Some assets have zero gains.
Buyer's Tax Ramifications	Assets get step-up in basis and start depreciating again. Plus, the buyer gets to depreciate purchased goodwill purchased.	Only get depreciation moving forward. Lose ability to depreciate goodwill purchased.	Assets get step-up in basis and start depreciating again. Plus, the buyer gets to depreciate purchased goodwill purchased.
Lease	Assumed by or assigned to the buyer. The seller remains on the lease until it expires, is renewed, or is released.	Requires landlord consent for new owner, and the personal guarantees of the seller need to be released.	Requires landlord consent for new owner, and the personal guarantees of the seller need to be released.
C-Corporation Double Tax	*Applies*	*Not applicable*	*Applies*
Capital Gains Tax	*Yes*	*Yes*	*Yes*
Ordinary Income Tax	*Yes*	*Not applicable*	*Yes*

Legal	Old company is shut down.	Old company continues in perpetuity. Legal purchase of the stock, membership, or partnership interest occurs.	Old company continues in perpetuity. Legal purchase of the stock, membership, or partnership interest occurs.
Risk to Seller	Less risk due to the entity being shut down.	The seller warranties the ongoing risk for past potential liability.	The seller warranties the ongoing risk for past potential liability.
Risk to Buyer	Very little	The seller warranties the ongoing risk for past potential liability.	The seller warranties the ongoing risk for past potential liability.
Documentation	Legal contracts are typically more complicated and lengthier.	Less complicated contracts, but representations and warranties are stricter.	Less complicated contracts, but representations and warranties are stricter. Wording for the election is added to the contract.
Representation and Warranties	*Regular*	*Extensive*	*Extensive*
Eligibility	*Any*	*Any*	Buyer and seller must both be corporations.
Representation and Warranties	*Regular*	*Extensive*	*Extensive*
Unique IRS Forms to File	*Form 4797 & Ord Inc.*	*Schedule D*	*Form 8023, 8883 Form 4797, and Ord Inc.*

For more information about the Section 338(h)(10) election, refer to Tony Nitti's article, "Tax Geek Tuesday: A Buyer's Best Friend - Understanding The Section 338(h)(10) Election," at forbes.com.

CHAPTER 16

When Is an Asset Sale Better Than a Stock Sale for a Seller?

When choosing between asset and stock sales, sellers usually push for a stock sale, and buyers typically push for an asset sale. As a seller, you need to know when to push for the sale and when not to push for it.

Let me give you an example to help you understand how it works. Let's assume that you are a medieval archer with only 10 arrows in your quiver. You have a battle with 10 people. Since you only have 10 arrows, you have to be very careful about when to use each one. If you use an arrow carelessly, it could cost you dearly.

Applying this example when negotiating with a buyer, if you know the buyer wants an asset sale and he or she thinks you want an entity sale, you can give the buyer that concession, which may be better for you. Then, in return, the buyer can give you another concession that makes you more money.

Understanding when an asset sale is better for you than a stock sale is paramount to maximizing your benefits in negotiation. But how do you know which one is better? How can you figure out when you should go for an asset sale or a stock sale?

The best way to figure it out is to consult your CPA or tax attorney before listing your business for sale and before signing the letter of intent. A good M&A advisor will point this out to you when he or she agrees to help you sell. As a general rule, if the sale of your business includes inventory and cash or working capital, an asset sale should be considered because it will put more money in your pocket after taxes.

The reason this works is that with an asset sale, you will have certain assets that will have zero taxable gain when you sell them. These assets include cash and inventory, which are sold at cost.

I suggest you consult with your M&A advisor and CPA in the early stages of the sales process to make sure you understand your tax burden under the differing sales structure types.

Why Consider an Asset Sale Structure?

The only way to honestly know which type of sales structure is best for you is to consult your M&A advisor and CPA before signing the letter of intent. Again, I suggest you consult with your M&A advisor and CPA in the early stages of the sales process to make sure you understand your tax burden under the differing sales structure types.

The following is an example of how an asset sale structure can save a seller $119,694 in taxes. The assets sold are cash, inventory, equipment, and goodwill, which are calculated as the difference between the book value of the assets and the purchase price.

		Asset Sale	Stock Sale
Cash		250,000	250,000
Inventory		1,250,000	1,250,000
Equipment		300,000	300,000
Retained Earnings		200,000	200,000
Total Assets		2,000,000	2,000,000
Purchase Price		5,000,000	5,000,000
Stock Basis		n/a	(500,000)
Capital Gain – Stock Sale			4,500,000
Capital Gain – Sale of Assets			
Cash	250,000		
Less: Basis	(250,000)		
Equals: Gain on Sale of Cash	-	-	

		Asset Sale	Stock Sale
Inventory	1,250,000		
Less: Basis	(1,2500,000)		
Equals: Gain on Sale of Inventory	-	-	
Ordinary Income on Equipment Sale		300,000	
Capital Gain on Goodwill Sold		3,200,000	
Total Amount Subject to Tax		3,500,000	4,500,000
Example of Tax			
	15%	60,270	60,270
	20%	627,946	819,640
Ordinary Income – Used 24%		72,000	-
		760,216	879,910
	Tax Savings with Asset Sale		**$119,694**

It is important to mention a scenario I came across when doing a stock sale makes more sense than doing an asset sale. One time, I was selling a same-day delivery business that had a fleet of vans, box trucks, and flatbed trucks. As we contemplated the deal structure and anticipated the impact of an asset sale on the buyer and seller, two factors arose that swayed the structure toward an asset sale, or Section 338(h)(10) sale:

1. Sales tax on the vehicles that the buyer would have to pay when he purchased the assets
2. Insurance premium increases

If we structured the sale as an asset sale, the fleet vehicles would need to be reregistered in the buyer's name. This would have cost the buyer over $100,000. If we did a stock sale, then the title to the vehicles wouldn't have changed hands, so the buyer wouldn't have to pay sales tax and reregister the vehicles.

The other consideration was insurance premium increases. The buyer had zero track record, so his insurance rates would have been high for several years until he could prove a good track record to the insurance company. The seller had an excellent track record, so he had the benefit of low insurance rates. If we did an asset sale, the insurance rates would start high, and the buyer would have to earn the lower rates over time. If we did a stock sale, the insurance rates would remain the same.

Additional Factors

There are additional factors that you, as a business owner, will need to be aware of that are specific to your industry and business, which can provide substantial tax-saving strategies. Consult with your CPA or tax attorney about specific factors that will impact your tax burden and which are unique to your industry or business.

CHAPTER 17

8 Common Types of Seller Compensation

As a certified Mergers & Acquisitions Professional (M&AP) representing sellers and buyers, I want to share eight of the most common types of compensation you can expect to be offered for the sale of a business and the advantages and disadvantages of each type. This chapter contains a numeric example of how the money would work for a sale based on a $1.5 million sales price for each of the eight most common ways a seller is compensated for the sale of a business:

- Cash
- Cash with Seller Note
- Earnout
- Profit-Sharing
- 100 Percent Seller Financing
- Board Membership Payment
- Consulting Fees
- Equity Rollover

Compensation Type 1: Cash

This is generally paid in full at close, but at a discount from the full asking price (usually 10 to 20 percent). You could expect to see $1,350,000 to $1,200,000 at close for a $1.5 million sales price, before taxes.

Advantages

It's quick, and you don't have to rely on a bank for funding. This is the cleanest structure, allowing a seller to get cash and not have to remain and worry about a seller note or earnout.

Disadvantages

Buyers generally aren't willing to pay full price for an all-cash structure.

Compensation Type 2: Cash with Seller Note

This type of structure involves a large down payment that is received at closing—typically 90 percent, but it could be less or more. You, as the seller, would act as the bank and finance the difference between the down payment and purchase price. This is called a seller note because you would hold a note payable to you for a specified amount, period, and interest rate. The payments received for the seller note will have an ordinary income component and a capital gains component over time, with note payments being treated like an installment sale.

I usually see a 10 percent seller note, so in this example, you would get $1,350,000 at close (for a $1.5 million sale) and be paid over time, generally three to five years for the remaining $150,000. If the interest rate is 6 percent, you, as the seller, will get paid $190,000 total. You would make more due to the interest received but have to wait three to five years for the remaining money before taxes.

Advantages

Sellers get more money for their business in the form of interest and can potentially save money on taxes due to the "installment sale" nature of receiving income over time versus all at one time, which usually throws you, as the seller, into the highest tax bracket.

Disadvantages

Buyers sometimes don't pay, and sellers run the risk of nonpayment. Sometimes the bank will require this note to be on "standby," meaning you can't be paid until the bank is paid in full or a specified amount of time has elapsed. The banks put this provision in as a protection to them. Banks are all about self-preservation.

Compensation Type 3: Earnout

The earnout structure allows you to share in future profits and potentially "earn" a higher amount from the sale of the business. This is usually done when the seller continues to work for the new owner. You don't share in the losses, but you don't have to put money into the company if there are losses, either. However, if there are losses, you don't get paid any earnout.

Depending on how this is worded, the income can be ordinary, capital gain, or both. It is usually not paid as W2 income to the seller.

This structure usually includes two payment types:

- Cash at closing
- An amount that is paid as it is "earned" over time based on a prescribed, agreed-upon metric

The cash at closing is usually at least 50 to 80 percent of the sales price, and the remainder is paid over a two-five-year time frame . The earnout portion is variable and theoretical; it could be zero, or it could be millions of dollars. There will be a time frame for the earnout, but I suggest not limiting the earnout (no cap) amount. Having no cap or ceiling may result in you getting *more* money for your business if there is explosive growth. If the buyer makes more money, then you do too. With a cap, you are disincentivized to grow the business above the capped amount of earnout.

It is important to note that it is highly preferential to have earnouts based on gross revenue or gross profit and not on net income. Basing the earnout on some "net" number leaves room for manipulation by the buyer to reduce the amount he or she has to pay the seller. Using a 50 percent down scenario, you would get $750,000 up front and be paid the rest after closing as it is earned, before taxes.

Advantages

- You could be paid much more for the business if you surpass the specified earnout amounts and payments.
- This usually works well when the owners are staying to work in the business and not retiring from it at closing.
- This allows a seller to share in future profits and growth after closing.

Disadvantages

Sellers have to wait to get paid. There aren't any guarantees of future payment except for the performance of the business. If the business does poorly under new management, you could very well get less money than the other options.

Compensation Type 4: Profit-Sharing

The profit-sharing structure is identical to the earnout structure except it is paid as W2 income and the income is taxed as ordinary income.

Compensation Type 5: 100 Percent Seller Financing

This is used most often for a partner buy-out or buy-in. Engineering, law, dental, and medical offices and CPA firms are the most common businesses that use this structure. It is a structure that allows senior partners to retain young, talented junior partners and have a built-in retirement plan for the senior partners.

The buyer gains ownership from the beginning, and his or her share of the profits are used to buy his or her share of the business. If you are financing 100 percent of the sale of your business, you will not receive any cash at closing.

One subset of this is when a seller will allow employees to own a small percentage of the company as a means to retain them. This ownership can be gifted, bought by the employee, or earned over time. This is similar to an employee stock ownership plan (ESOP), only less complicated and less costly, and less of an administrative burden is borne by the seller.

Advantages

A purchaser can own a business with little or zero down payment. The sales price is established based on some set criteria negotiated and can be higher than the market price. Since you would be receiving payments over time, you would be eligible for installment sale taxes, which allows you to take advantage of the tiered tax structure.

Disadvantages

- You get paid over time versus up front on an installment sale basis, thus potentially reducing your taxes.
- You may not get paid at all. You will want to have some clawback provisions in the contract to allow you to regain control if the payments aren't made.
- You lose management control if you sell 100 percent all at once.

Compensation Type 6: Board Membership Payment

Board membership payment is a way for you to be compensated in the future for services rendered and remain involved in the strategic decisions of the company. You don't have to work for the buyer in any other capacity but can choose to work for the buyer in addition to being a board member. This right has no ownership and can be given in addition to any of the previous compensation packages mentioned here. Income received from being a board member is ordinary income.

Advantages

Sitting on an advisory board of directors and being compensated for it is a way to retain some level of influence of the future operation of the business. It is particularly helpful when you are still being paid on a seller note.

Disadvantages

You don't have a clean break, and you still have to think about the business after closing.

Compensation Type 7: Consulting Fees

Consulting fees are what you charge while working for the buyer as a subcontractor, as needed, for the buyer on a consulting basis. If this compensation structure is agreed upon, the hourly rate paid to the seller is usually specified in the purchase agreement. Payments received as a consultant are ordinary income.

Advantages

Consulting agreements can be used to supplement deferred or standby payments on the seller note, thus allowing you to still have an income stream when the bank won't allow note payments to be made.

Disadvantages

You need to work to earn the consulting fees and still be involved in the business after closing.

Compensation Type 8: Equity Rollover

You may choose to roll over a part of your equity or convert your seller note to equity (convertible debentures) to continue to own a part of the company. This ownership is usually as a minority owner, so you would relinquish the rights of majority ownership to the buyer. With this structure, you would have shared ownership responsibilities and obligations along with the buyer after closing.

The equity rollover structure allows you to take a large chunk of money at closing and, potentially, cash another significant check when the company sells a second time. After closing, you can continue to work for the company or not. Your specific role and compensation are negotiated as part of the sales process.

Advantages

This can be a way for you to potentially get another large payment when the business is sold again.

Disadvantages

You may not get more money if the business fails.

WHAT INCREASES THE VALUE OF MY BUSINESS BEFORE I SELL?

CHAPTER 18

Top 8 Value Drivers of Business

What are value drivers? They are key elements of your business and the sales process that will either increase or decrease the value of your business and the amount of money you put in your pocket when you sell. If you are considering a sale of your business or are just curious, these can be used as benchmarks and key performance indicators (KPI) to help you increase the value of your business.

For years, I've recorded what buyers like and don't like to see and what motivates them to pay more for a business than they normally would. It is important to you as a seller to identify these factors. The earlier you can start working on them, the better off you will be.

Here are eight key value drivers:

- Market Timing vs. My Timing
- Financial Performance
- Management
- Proprietary Assets
- Customer Concentration
- Opportunity/Runway
- Uniqueness and Competitiveness
- A Good Story

Value Driver 1: Market Timing vs. My Timing

Clients often ask me when the best time is to sell their business. I tell them that it's not as much about market timing as it is your timing. You'll find that listing your business based solely on market timing is a fruitless endeavor. List your business when your business is ready to be listed. What I mean by that is you have one chance to make a first impression with the buyer pool, so do it right. Making a good first impression is one way to optimize the selling price. Take the time you need to prepare so that when you list your business for sale, you don't just list it—you launch it.

It's not as much about market timing as it is your timing.

| Don't just list it: LAUNCH it.

Value Driver 2: Financial Performance

When a financial buyer is contemplating a purchase, the number one metric he or she will use to measure value is financial performance. EBITDA and SDE (seller's discretionary earnings) are two key metrics to focus on increasing. If your business has sales of less than $1 million, the multiple most widely used is SDE. If your business has sales over $1 million, your multiple is EBITDA. If your business is a dental office or CPA firm, your multiple is revenue. Since revenue, EBITDA, or SDE have an exponential impact on the selling price of your business, you will want to carefully monitor these to maximize selling price prior to and during the sales process.

Revenue, EBITDA, and SDE are key financial performance value drivers.

Most businesses sell as a multiple of these numbers. Minimize all nonessential expenses. Deposit all cash you receive. I can't believe I'm saying this, but you may have to pay more taxes to gain more later. Let's say our business sells for 4x of EBITDA. This means for every additional dollar of EBITDA, you will get $4 more of selling price. Increasing EBITDA gives you a 400 percent return on your money. That's a good investment. If you choose to take unnecessary expenses—say, for $100—then you save $35 of taxes (assuming you are in the 35 percent federal and state tax bracket). Would you rather have an additional $35 or an additional $300?

Financial Advantage

Not only do you want to monitor key financial metrics, but it is also important that the financial information being presented is accurate. This involves taking time to get your financials in order to ensure the financial part of your offering will shine. A lot of sellers fall short here. You will have a financial advantage over other businesses for sale by presenting good financial information to the buyers in a timely fashion. Are your books accurate and up to date? Do you report on a GAAP- or cash-basis? If so, then GAAP is preferred. It is not as important for transactions lower than $1 million.

Other financial metrics to keep an eye on are capital expenditures (CapEx). Keep working capital at a minimum, sell unused or stale inventory, and actively collect on aged receivables. Ensure that your CapEx supports your growth model. Reduce the need for working capital to clean things up before you sell to reduce that requirement at closing. All these items will influence the selling price of your business negatively or positively.

High Gross Profit Margins

One other key value driver is profit margin. Buyers like and are willing to pay more for businesses with high profit margins.

What about financial trends? Are there patterns of growth or decline in your business? If in decline, are there good reasons for the decline? Detailing these reasons is crucial. Accurate and up-to-date accrual and GAAP-basis financials are important for a buyer to determine how the company rates in its industry and amongst competitors. A comparison to industry ratios can identify strengths and weaknesses in the business. These factors have a significant impact on business value.

Value Driver 3: Management

What is the experience level of the current management team? How long have they been with the business? Are they planning to retire soon? These are common questions asked by buyers who are looking at a business.

> The business needs to run better in your absence than your presence.

Buyers often want to see an organization chart detailing key management personnel. The better the management, the higher the price tends to be. Also, if the business runs better in your absence than in your presence, it will be valued higher. What is the average length of employment amongst your staff? A responsible business buyer will be looking for opportunities where the current staff, especially management, will remain in place following your exit from the business.

Prospective buyers want to see contracts for key employees and noncompete agreements reflected in the business evaluation. More importantly, they're looking for signs of a loyal, dedicated staff that is committed to the company's success regardless of ownership change.

Value Driver 4: Proprietary Assets

If proprietary assets such as patents are included, they increase the value and price of the business. These assets are often valued individually within the business valuation. Has your company developed a unique application, software, tool, or technology as part of its ongoing operations? Does it give you a competitive advantage? If so, this proprietary innovation or intellectual property can be positioned as a key value driver for your business. Technologies or processes do not have to be patented to carry value, but privacy and confidentiality must be maintained. It is critical that noncompete and confidentiality agreements be strictly adhered to and enforced by the company before and after a transfer of ownership. The benefits, application, and purpose of your proprietary technology should be explained to a business valuation expert.

Proprietary assets may also give you a technological advantage over your competitors. These include software and technology but also include processes and internal systems. I met with a seller who developed ways to manufacture a product in less than half the time of the competition. He had a team of engineers who had figured out how to minimize the assembly and construction times of the machines he made to reduce costs. This was a technological advantage that he had and could sell.

Intangibles, or intellectual property and human resources, can be protected and leveraged through a combination of business strategies and legal protections. Business strategies include incentive compensation plans to recognize, reward, and retain high-performing employees. Legal protections include requiring key employees to sign noncompete agreements, registering trademarks and copyrights, and taking steps to protect proprietary information/trade secrets such as recipes and formulas. Contracts with key players—including partners, customers, and suppliers—are also important.

Value Driver 5: Customer Concentration

Customer concentration is calculated as the revenue earned from each customer as a percentage of total revenue. A low concentration of customers (customer concentration), when no single customer comprises more than 5 to 10 percent of revenue, is optimal. Retail stores have few problems with customer concentration because they typically have a lot of customers. Service or product-based businesses, on the other hand, can struggle to keep a low customer concentration.

Low levels of customer concentration are favorable to a higher value of the business. If we created a pie chart of revenue contributed by each customer, the optimal low customer concentration would look like this:

Revenue Contributed by Each Customer (Low Concentration)

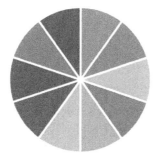

High customer concentration is a negative value driver that you need to be aware of. It impacts value negatively due to the risk imposed by a business having a single customer who can be lost, which loss would be devastating to the revenue of the business. Do you have one or two major customers that account for more than 25 percent of your gross sales? What would happen to the value of your company if you lost one?

A good overview and a rating analysis of your customer base can be beneficial for added value. It can also provide valuable insight for where, how, and when you advertise—not to mention a much better understanding of your accounts receivable and aging.

The pie chart for a high customer concentration looks more like this:

Revenue Contributed by Each Customer (High Concentration)

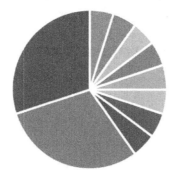

Value Driver 6: Opportunity/Runway

The opportunity of the business tends to be a value driver for strategic buyers. Strategic buyers buy a business based more on what they can do with the business than what the numbers show. An example of this would be a business buying out a competitor to increase market share.

Companies also grow through vertical integration and acquisition of suppliers and customers. If you will take the time to paint a picture of how exponential growth could occur with increased capital and expertise, this will prove to be a powerful selling tool to impress buyers. I would recommend being specific with projections based on growth for every additional dollar spent and what those funds would be used to buy.

Value Driver 7: Uniqueness and Competitiveness

Having a distinct advantage over your competition is an important value driver for your business. What makes your business unique? What edge do you have over competitors? This can be the fact that you are married to the daughter of the largest customer (which wouldn't give you a higher selling price).

Here are some examples of competitive advantages:

- Providing a unique service or product
- Expertise in a specialized field
- Proprietary software that you developed and use
- The ability to source raw materials
- Exclusive customer or vendor contracts
- Opportune location
- Master service agreements that are no longer available
- Long-term leases that are locked in with below-market lease rates

Define what makes you unique and what edges you hold over everyone else. Making sure the buyer is aware of these keen advantages is an important part of the sales process. You may not recognize what your advantages are, but take time to discover them so you can highlight them to your buyers. For the advantage to be valuable, it must be transferable.

For the advantage to be valuable, it must be transferable.

What do you do better than the competition? There are two types of competition that impact selling price. The first is your competitive advantage. The second is the competitive landscape. Highly competitive market segments tend to suppress prices, while fragmented markets with little competition tend to bring premium prices. Does your company compete in a clearly defined market niche that is defensible? Or, have your products or services become a commodity that is becoming more difficult to defend?

Value Driver 8: A Good Story

For your business to sell for more money, you and your advisor must accurately convey the business model to the buyer. Tell a good story. Buyers need to clearly understand the business in order to buy it. A confused buyer is going to keep looking for a business that makes sense.

A good business story will include descriptions of the following:

- Business model
- Customer acquisition and retention
- Revenue streams
- Marketing
- Employees
- Management

Buyers need to be able to either see themselves replacing the owner or their people replacing the owner. It is like test-driving a car. Buyers want to sit, see, feel, and understand how it all works to buy. Tell a good story, and you will get more for your business as buyers clearly see the value.

CHAPTER 19

What You Need to Know about Accounting

I recently joked with a seller that he was quickly becoming more of an accountant than he wanted to be. All kidding aside, this is partially true. You don't need to know everything about accounting to sell your business for top dollar, but there are vital things you must know and understand. This chapter will teach you precisely what you need to know about accounting and how the game is played to maximize the selling price of your business. Most importantly, you will learn how to utilize multiple arbitrages to maximize the selling price of your business.

Maximize Net Income to Sell

Like any entrepreneur, you have sought to minimize taxes for as long as you have owned the business. Every year, you've hired a CPA or tax advisor to help you prepare those taxes to minimize your tax burden. This works for Uncle Sam, but it is not what you want to do when selling your business. Instead, you want your net income to be as high as it can be. With this in mind, you will need to identify what expenses you can remove to increase your net income. With EBITDA, it is easy; you take out interest, taxes (income), depreciation, and amortization. When calculating SDE or adjusted EBITDA, it is a different story.

> When running a business, you MINIMIZE net income. When selling a business, you MAXIMIZE it.

What Is Discretionary?

I have written a lot about discretionary expenses. Discretionary expenses are valid expenses that you choose to incur that the new owner won't necessarily have. Identifying discretionary expenses is critical because you can remove these from the profit and loss statement, thus increasing your net income. Here is a list of common discretionary expenses:

Owner Expenses

- Wages
- Payroll taxes, employer portion
- Health insurance
- Life insurance
- Automobile
- Cell phone
- 401(k), pension plan, or retirement plan employer contributions
- Perks, like golf memberships, sporting tickets, etc.
- Meals, food, and beverage
- Cost of continuing education for a dentist, engineer, or doctor
- Any other expense paid on the owner's behalf

Other Business-Related Expenses

- Loss on the sale of assets
- Lawsuit expenses, settlement expenses, or payouts
- One-time bad-debt write-off
- Lease expense to market (if the seller owns the building)

One-Time Income That Needs to Be Excluded

- Gain on the sale of assets
- One-time payments received
- Income from extraordinary events that aren't expected to reoccur
- CAPEX needs to be considered, if applicable

It is essential to identify these expenses for each of the previous three years and the current year so your advisor can calculate SDE, EBITDA, and adjusted EBITDA.

Multiple Arbitrage

Multiple arbitrage is a concept that, when applied correctly, allows you to exponentially increase the selling price of your business. Here is how it works: For every dollar you increase SDE and EBITDA, you exponentially increase the value of your business.

> Use multiple arbitrage to maximize your selling price.

Here is an example of the calculation: Let's assume that your business uses a multiple of 4x EBITDA to calculate value. If your EBITDA is $500,000, then your value is $2,000,000. If your EBITDA increases $100,000 to $600,000, then your value goes to $2,400,000. The extra $100,000 of EBITDA gave you an extra $400,000 of value. With this example, it is like investing $1 to gain $4. Where else can you get a 400 percent return on your money?

CHAPTER 20

It's All about Risk

There are six types of risks that can impact the salability and price of your business. The higher the risk, the more pressure there is for a seller to decrease the selling price of their business.

You should assess each of the following risks when considering the sale of your business:

1. Quality of Financial Information Risk

2. Diversification Risk

3. Management Risk

4. Industry-Inherent Risks

5. Competition Risk

6. Time-in-Business Risk

> The higher the risk, the lower the price.

Quality of Financial Information Risk

The buyer's level of confidence in the information provided is known as the quality of financial information. Audited financials are required to produce the highest level of confidence in the financial report. Financials created internally offer the lowest level of confidence. Reviewed and compiled financials are the next-best type of financial information provided by you as a seller.

Diversification Risk

The less diversified a business is, the higher the risk to the buyers. Diversification risk has three main components:

1. Suppliers

How diverse are the key suppliers? If one supplier went out of business, how would the business replace that supplier? Would it disrupt the revenue stream?

2. Products/Services

How diverse are the products and services of the business? What percentage of revenue is derived from a single product or service? If that product or service were discontinued, how would that affect revenue?

3. Location (Geographic Location)

What susceptibilities exist due to the physical location of the business? Is the business in a poor location that could be improved?

Management Risk

If management were to leave the business, it would impact revenue and earnings before interest, taxes, depreciation, and amortization (EBITDA). The risk of the negative impact on the financials is known as management risk. Management risk includes the reliance upon the current owner(s) and management of the business to run the business. The more likely the business will be impacted if the owner leaves, the higher the management risk. This is also true of key employees and customers as well. If the current management is in place and the owner only provides strategic oversight, this is the lowest level of management risk.

Industry-Inherent Risks

What is the industry like? Is the industry in infancy stages, or is it mature? Is the industry volatile? Is it risky by nature? These key components impact the industry risk and the selling price of the business.

Competition Risk

Industries with a fiercely competitive landscape tend to have higher competition risk. The higher the competition risk, the lower the price of the goods and services provided. Lower profit margins mean lower EBITDA and selling price.

Time-in-Business Risk

Businesses tend to have a higher rate of failure in the first five years of inception, so the longer the business has been in operation, the less time in business risk you have.

It is difficult to quantify the impact that risk factors can have on the selling price of your business. However, when the risk factors are high, it is safe to say they will negatively impact the selling price of your business or require a more creative payment structure to you as the seller.

If you can reduce the risk for any or all of these six risks prior to taking your business to market, it will bring you a higher selling price as the buyer gains confidence in his or her ability to scale the business moving forward.

TAXES AND HOW TO MINIMIZE

CHAPTER 21

Structuring a Sale to Minimize Your Taxes

In the past, when a seller asked me about taxes, my answer was simple: "I'm sorry, but you have to pay them."

Fortunately, you now have a handful of tax-reduction strategies at your disposal that can potentially reduce your tax burden. These include the following:

- CAPS Trust/Asset Exchange Structure
- CRT/CRAT/CRUT
- Charitable Gifting of Stock
- QSBS IRS Section 1202 Exclusion of Income
- Opportunity Zones
- ESOP
- Cooperative Conversions

This chapter is designed to introduce you to these tax-saving strategies so you can decide whether to seek further guidance from one of the advisors who specialize in them. Each of these strategies has unique, complicated laws and rules that apply; it is only with the help of an expert that you can fully understand and determine which ones work for you.

CPAs and tax attorneys aren't exposed to many of the tax-saving strategies.

People ask me why more people don't know about these strategies. Typically, the answer comes down to three reasons:

1. The strategies are highly specialized and require in-depth knowledge.
2. In the normal course of business, CPAs and tax advisors aren't exposed to these strategies. The application of these strategies is not one that people encounter often. Therefore, they require a professional who is regularly exposed to tax strategies involving business sales.
3. You need money to be exposed to these strategies, and many sellers haven't had enough money to necessitate this level of advice and service prior to selling their business.

It is important to remember that obscurity doesn't diminish legitimacy. Understanding and utilizing these strategies is crucial to your success. In Chapter 23, you'll find a list of people you can contact to learn more about each of these strategies as you seek to learn which one or ones are right for you.

CAPS Trust/Asset Exchange Structure

With a CAPS trust/asset exchange structure, there is a buyer and a seller, just like a conventional sale. However, the business or real estate is sold to an unrelated third party (the trust, Sale 1), which immediately sells to the buyer (Sale 2). From a buyer's perspective, it is seamless: The buyer purchases the business under the same terms, only it is purchased from "XYZ Trust" instead of "ABC Seller."

From a seller's perspective, the transaction is structured as an installment sale under IRS Section 453, whereby the asset is first sold to an unrelated third party (irrevocable trust) in exchange for a secured installment note. This note is flexible in payment and terms, so the seller can determine his or her cash flow needs on a monthly basis and structure the payments based on those needs. The note creates an income stream for the seller, secured by the assets of the trust, that gets taxed as the seller receives the income like an installment sale, governed by installment sale tax law.

When the business or real estate is sold to the irrevocable trust, the taxes are deferred (not eliminated) for the seller. Deferment is the postponement or delay of paying the capital gains tax since the sale of the business or real estate is a taxable event. The trust proceeds can be invested in stocks, bonds, marketable securities, annuities, life insurance policies, etc., to provide income to the seller, which is paid through the note.

This strategy offers the following benefits:

- You can sell your business, put more money to work, and *pay less in taxes over time* instead of all at once.
- Pretax dollars are utilized over time to maximize returns.
- Business owners can sell their business and defer the taxes on capital gains for up to 20 years.
- Real estate owners can sell real estate and defer the taxes on capital gains for up to 20 years.
- Sellers can put up to 45 percent more money in their pocket.
- The strategy can serve as an alternative for or rescue from a 1031 exchange.
- This strategy can service transactions over $1 million.
- C-corporation owners can reduce double taxation.
- As an estate planning/asset protection tool, the trust provides *valuable protection* of the proceeds received from the sale.

The CAPS trust structure is a powerful tax reduction tool for two reasons:

- The seller receives the use of "before tax" proceeds for up to 20 years to put more money in his or her pocket. Normally, the seller would be forced to pay 100 percent of the taxes in full up front. Instead, sellers can use these funds to make money over time— even enough money to pay the taxes in the future as it is paid out of the trust.
- It allows the seller to plan when the taxes are paid and take advantage of tiered tax rates. A seller can effectively lower his or her tax rates on some of the tax that would have been due if the taxes were all paid at close.

For more information about the CAPS/asset exchange structures, visit capstrust.org or assetexchangeexperts.com.

CRT/CRAT/CRUT

CRTs, CRATs, and CRUTs (charitable remainder trusts, charitable remainder annuity trusts, and charitable remainder unitrusts, respectively) are tax-exempt, irrevocable trusts designed and established to reduce taxable income for a seller with a charitable purpose in mind. These structures allow a seller to donate highly appreciated assets to an irrevocable trust, pay zero tax when the assets are sold, and create income over the lifetime of the seller.

There are two types of remainder trusts that distribute income to the seller:

- A fixed amount (annuity) is distributed each year.
- A fixed percentage is distributed each year based on the balance of the trust assets.

Income is dispersed to the beneficiaries for a specified period, and the remainder (of at least 10 percent of the statistical fair market value of the contributed property) is donated to a designated qualified charity.

Since the trust receives the assets at fair market value, there is no gain or loss within the trust when the assets are sold. The trust then invests the proceeds from the sale of the contributed assets in income-producing assets. The seller is also the donor to the trust and is entitled to a charitable deduction based on the present value of the remainder interest in the trust.

These structures work well for sellers who want to pursue philanthropic goals while generating income. These vehicles are commonly used for retirement and estate planning.

The use of a CRT trust is appealing for the following reasons:

- The seller gets the use of pretax dollars to invest over time.
- A charity gets a large donation.
- The seller gets a lifetime income stream and pays taxes on an installment basis versus a lump-sum basis.
- An immediate charitable deduction is allowed for a portion of the gift when the assets are donated to the trust.

- The assets are protected within the trust from outside creditors.

This type of structure comes with its share of limitations:

- The seller needs to show a charitable purpose prior to executing an LOI, so proper planning is imperative.
- Compared to other structures, the seller receives far less money over his or her lifetime due to the charity receiving the remainder.
- Once the assets are donated to the trust, the seller relinquishes all rights of ownership to the trust moving forward. The transfer is irrevocable, and the terms are not flexible.
- The annual payments terminate upon the death of the seller/ donor or the contracted term (whichever comes first). If the seller dies prematurely, his or her heirs lose the benefit of the income stream. To mitigate this risk, the structure is often combined with life insurance to pay the beneficiaries in case of the early, untimely death of the seller/donor.

QUICK GUIDE
Comparative Analysis

NUMERIC EXAMPLE			
	Sell Outright, No Tax Deferral	CRT/CRAT/ CRUT Trust	CAPS Trust
Sales Price	$1,500,000	$1,500,000	$1,500,000
Appraised Value of Stock (estimated)	–	$1,400,000	Not applicable
Basis	$0	$0	$0
Charitable Deduction Year 1	Not applicable	$534,000	$0
Tax Reduction Year 1	Not applicable	$240,000	$0
Tax Due after Closing (estimated 25%)	$375,000	$0	Taxed on ordinary income; capital gains deferred
Remaining Cash	$1,125,000	–	–
Annual Cash Flow (estimated 5% after fees)	$56,250	$75,000	$75,000
20-Year Annual Cash Flow	$1,125,000	$1,500,000	$1,500,000
Principal or Original Amount Put into the Trust Returned to Seller	$1,500,000	Partial beneficial interest in the future value***	$1,500,000
Total Cash Flow to Seller over 20 Years (annual + year 1 tax reduction + principal)	$2,625,000	$1,740,000	$3,000,000
Amount Given to a Charity	$0	$1,500,000	$0
Setup Cost	$0	$2,000–$10,000	1%
Annual Cost to Administer	$0	0.5%–1%	0.625%
Annual Appraisal Cost	$0	$2,500–$7,500	$0
Termination Cost	$0	1%–5%	$0

QUICK GUIDE
Comparative Analysis
QUESTIONS

	Sell Outright, No Tax Deferral	CRT/CRAT/ CRUT Trust	CAPS Trust
What if the seller wants to take additional payments annually or the seller's needs change?	*Allowed*	*Not allowed*	Allowed, though the seller pays taxes on what is withdrawn.
What if the seller dies before 20 years?	Heirs get the cash.	The trust goes to the heirs as specified in the will.	The trust goes to the heirs as specified in the will.
How are the annual payments taxed?	Payments are taxed as either ordinary income or capital gains, depending on the type of income.	Payments are taxed as either ordinary income or capital gains, depending on the type of income.***	Payments are taxed as either ordinary income or capital gains, depending on the type of income.
What is the required minimum annual payout?	*Flexible*	*5%*	*3.5% (AFR)*
What is the maximum annual payout?	*Unlimited*	*50%*	*Unlimited*
What happens when the seller dies?	Benefit goes to the heirs.	Annual payments are paid for the seller's life or up to 20 years.	Annual payments are paid to the heirs as specified in the will.
What types of investments are allowed?	*Any*	*Any, with limitations**	*Stocks, bonds, life Insurance*
What is the max time to payout?	*None*	*Lifetime or 20 years*	*None*
What is the required minimum term for the trust?	*None*	*Two years*	None. However, three years is preferable since there is a setup cost.
What is the year 1 income tax deduction?	*None*	*20–50%*	*None*

What is the year 1 reduction in taxes?	*None*	*10–35%*	*None*
What if gains in the trust exceed disbursements?	*Not applicable*	*Limited benefit***	Benefit goes to the seller at the end of the note term.
How do I determine annual income received?	This is up to the seller.	This is based on a formula or the trust documents when it is set up. It will either be a percentage of the value of the trust or a fixed amount.	The seller determines his or her needs when the trust is set up, and the note is structured around those needs.
Can my minimum annual payments go down?	*Yes*	*Yes, if the value decreases*	*Not unless the note is refinanced or value decreases*
Is there a fixed term?	*Not applicable*	*20 years or the lifetime of the designee*	The note is set up with a fixed term but can be refinanced to extend the term. There is no limitation on the number of years, although most people want it to be between five and 20 years.
Can you add additional assets to the trust?	*Not applicable*	*Yes*	*Yes*
Who is the trustee?	*Not applicable*	*May be the seller**	*Third-party licensed trust company*
Can the trustee be replaced?	*Not applicable*	*Yes*	*Yes*
Who makes investment decisions?	*The seller*	*May be the seller**	A registered investment advisor makes the decisions with input from the seller.
Does this provide asset protection?	*No*	*Yes*	*Yes*

*CRTs are complicated to administer and subject to various federal and state rules governing charitable trusts. The donor may feel that it is not time well spent to learn these rules, especially given the penalties for errors. Investments must have diversity and marketability. The trustee must make investments that are prudent.

**With a unitrust, the beneficiary gets a percentage of the total trust (it must be valued annually) distributed annually, so only a portion of gains are distributed. The trust is designed to leave money to the charity. Other types of CRTS allow for a fixed amount to be distributed over time.

***The seller makes a gift of the property to the CRUT and receives a partial beneficial interest in the future value of the trust. The tax allocation rules for CRTs are complex. Typically, the trust administrator provides these calculations; almost all CRT trustees will hire a company specializing in this for the term of the trust.

Each form of trust has limitations and strict rules, so consult with your advisor. This site contains some good information for you to learn more: estateplanning.com/Understanding-Charitable-Remainder-Trusts/.

Charitable Gifting of Stock

This tax-saving structure allows charitable-minded sellers to give more money to a charity than they would if they merely sold their business, paid the tax, and gifted the net amount to a charity. It allows a seller to gift stock, membership, or partnership interests to a charity at market value, thus giving the seller a charitable deduction for tax purposes and eliminating capital gains for the seller for the gift. It does not eliminate the tax for the charity; it reduces the overall amount of taxes paid by both the seller and charity when the business is sold.

Here is how it works: You set up an account for gifting with an investment advisor that is funded with the gifted stock, membership interest, or partnership interest that you donate to the account. The account is set up as a 501(c)3 public charity. The stock, membership, or partnership interests you want to transfer are transferred into the account you set up. This asset is then sold by the charity to the buyer. Since the charity you donate the stock to is a 501(c)3 public charity, the charity does not pay taxes on the sale of the stock. The charity does, however, pay an unrelated business income tax (UBIT) on the income derived while the stock is owned and on gains derived when the stock is sold. This tax is paid with the proceeds from the sale of the stock. You get to treat the market value of your investment as a charitable deduction in the year of the gift. This strategy works with C corporations, S corporations, LLCs, and partnerships.

This comes with three main benefits:

1. You receive a charitable deduction for the fair market value of the stock or interest donated in the year of the gift.
2. Capital gains are eliminated for the value of the gifted stock or interest.
3. For the charitably minded person, this is a way to give more to the charity than you would if you were to sell, pay the tax, and donate the after-tax proceeds.

Here is an example of how the numbers work and the benefits derived from this strategy:

	Sell $1,000,000 Outright	Gift $1,000,000 to Charity
Long-Term Capital Gains to Be Paid	$238,000	$0
Effective UBIT Paid	$0	$100,000
Discount Applied Due to Lack of Control and Minority Interest	5–10%	$20,000
Charitable Deduction	$762,000	$1,020,000 (includes discount)
Amount Available to Give to Charity	$762,000	$900,000
Additional Amount Available to Give to Charity	$138,000	

QSBS IRS Section 1202 Exclusion of Income

QSBS stands for qualified small business stock, which falls under Section 1202 of the IRS code. Section 1202 was enacted in 1993 to incentivize taxpayers to invest in certain small businesses. Both the seller and the buyer need to meet strict criteria for the exclusion to apply.

The statute allows for a taxpayer to exclude the gains realized from the sale or exchange of QSBS stock for certain C corporations held for more than five years as follows:

- 50 percent exclusion for QSBS acquired prior to February 18, 2009
- 75 percent exclusion for QSBS acquired between February 18, 2009, and September 27, 2010
- 100 percent exclusion for QSBS acquired after September 27, 2010

There are many limitations, including thresholds of $10 million and $50 million, so consult your tax advisor about this strategy. C corporations that involve the performance of services in health, law, engineering, brokerages, financial services, architecture, consulting, athletics, banking, insurance, financing, leasing, farming, oil, and gas are specifically excluded. The laws and regulations for this exclusion are complex, so you will want to make sure you hire a good attorney or CPA who is familiar with IRS Section 1202. For the lucky few, this strategy works well for reducing taxes on the sale of stock.

Opportunity Zones

In 2018, 8,766 opportunity zones were enacted to encourage long-term private capital investments in low-income communities in all 50 states ("Opportunity Zones," Economic Innovation Group, eig.org/opportunityzones/facts-and-figures).

These are designed to help these communities through outside investment and benefit the investor with tax breaks. This help comes in the form of job creation and economic development due to the creation of the opportunity zones. If you buy a business that is in one of the opportunity zones, you get future tax breaks when you sell and can eliminate your capital gains if you've held the business asset for at least 10 years.

Individual taxpayers can establish an opportunity fund if they follow the guidelines set by the IRS. Taxpayers are granted a temporary deferral of inclusion in the taxable income for capital gains that are reinvested in an opportunity fund. This is valid until December 31, 2026. Taxpayers also receive a step-up in a basis of 10 percent if the investment is held for at least five years and 15 percent is held for seven years, which further reduces the tax burden by excluding the basis gained. If the investment is held for at least 10 years, 100 percent of the capital gains is excluded when the assets are sold. The exclusion applies to gains on accrued investments made in the opportunity fund and does not apply to the initial deferred gain (Steve Bertoni, "An Unlikely Group Of Billionaires And Politicians Has Created The Most Unbelievable Tax Break Ever," Forbes, July 18, 2018).

You are probably wondering how this will help you as a seller. As a seller in an opportunity zone, your business has just become much more attractive to buyers. If your business isn't in an opportunity zone, you can still defer your gains if you buy real estate or another business located within one.

ESOP

Employee stock option plans (ESOPs) were sanctioned by the Employee Retirement Income Security Act (ERISA) starting in 1974. An ESOP is a qualified defined contribution retirement plan where the assets of the plan are invested in the seller's (sponsoring company's) stock. ESOPs provide tax advantages, including a reduction in capital gains and a deferment of capital gains, up to 100 percent in the event of the death of the seller prior to the proceeds of the sale having been disqualified from IRS Section 1042 capital gains protection.

ESOPs are a good fit when the following apply:

- You have a business value of at least $5 million or a net income of at least $1 million.
- Strong management is in place.
- There are more than 20 full-time employees.
- There is a five-year history of profitable operations.
- A seller wants to attract, retain, and reward the employees by offering ownership of the business.
- Strong financials can be produced that can be used to obtain financing.

ESOPs are not a good fit when the following apply:

- A seller wants to liquidate and get the majority of his or her money at closing.
- Complex reporting and annual costs exceed the benefits derived from the ESOP.

For more information about ESOPs, visit suncrestadvisors.com/could-an-esop-be-your-exit-strategy/.

Cooperative Conversions

This type of sales structure is somewhat like an ESOP, except it is typically used for businesses that are too small or are otherwise not a fit for an ESOP structure. A cooperative is member-owned and democratically controlled, based on an equitable patronage system. The business can be sold to employees, suppliers, customers, or a combination of these. This structure offers employees the opportunity for profit sharing. Profits are distributed based on an equitable patronage system. There are four types of cooperative conversion:

1. Conversion of the original entity to a cooperative (**Straight Conversion**)
2. Formation of a new entity to acquire the business assets (**Asset Sale**)
3. Formation of a new entity to acquire the original entity (**Stock Sale**)
4. Formation of a new entity that merges with the original entity (**Merger**)

Bank or seller financing is used for the purchase under each type of cooperative. Cooperative conversions generally share the same tax consequences as a traditional sale, unlike the ESOP. For more information, visit rmeoc.org/become-employee-owned/colorado-employee-owned/.

MANAGING AND CHOOSING YOUR ADVISORY TEAM

CHAPTER 22

Legal Stage of the Transaction: Attorneys and Fences

This chapter is about protecting yourself against threats to the transaction during the legal phase of the process. The concept of protection may seem a bit odd, but it is necessary. You will also learn how not to let your legal fees become exorbitant and lower your stress level. I will outline three crucial fences you will need to install to protect your transaction. Finally, you will learn two bonus strategies for negotiating the sticky points of the legal process.

Now that you have nearly completed due diligence and are anticipating a closing in the next few weeks, it is time to march into the legal phase of the sales process. You may have worked for months to get to this point. You and the buyer are excited to work together and move forward. At this stage of the transaction, you may get what we call deal fatigue. You get a little tired of the whole sales process. Both sides are anxious to get the transaction closed and funded so you can both move on to better things. There is a tendency to want to turn things over to the attorneys to wrap things up, leaving you to move on to more pressing matters, like running your business.

This is precisely what you DON'T want to do! You must take control and not turn the steering wheel over entirely to the attorneys. Here is an example of why this is true.

I live on a small ranch. One year, I decided to grow a large garden. We had to till the ground, fertilize, and plant seeds to hopefully harvest in the fall. My wife and I spent a lot of time that summer working in the garden. One of the crops we planted was strawberries. After a lot of hard work, blood, sweat, and tears, we watched the berries form on the stems and finally start to ripen. We were excited and looking forward to the harvest.

Shortly afterward, the local mule deer herd discovered our strawberry patch and quickly went to work, eating the berries, trampling the plants, and destroying our hard work. We were on the cusp of a bountiful harvest when all our hard work was nearly destroyed by outside animals! It took a lot of additional work to get back to the point we were at before and finally harvest. Once we learned of this threat, we installed a high fence around the garden and didn't have any more problems with the deer.

So goes the sale of a business. We spend weeks and sometimes months with the buyer, and a relationship, even a friendship, is nurtured and developed between the buyer and seller. Trust is gained, and there is usually a mutual liking for each other that occurs. The process of drafting and finalizing the legal documents necessary for closing is a critical phase of the transaction because the transaction is vulnerable to attacks by well-meaning attorneys and CPAs. The transaction can easily turn from sensational to adversarial without the fences I will mention. It also needs to be carefully piloted by a good advisor. This phase is where your advisor will earn his or her money and create value by keeping the transaction on the rails.

At this point, we are ready to turn over the transaction to the legal teams to draft documents and get the transaction closed. This is where, like the deer in my garden, all the hard work up to that point can get destroyed. Feelings can get trampled on, people can easily get at odds with each other, and the transaction becomes tenuous, even in jeopardy of not closing at all. All of this is due to well-meaning attorneys (CPAs as well, sometimes) who can put people at odds with each other and turn the transaction from collaborative to confrontational.

Just like I did with my garden, you need to put up fences to protect the transaction and yourself against threats to the transaction.

Why is the legal phase of the transaction so vulnerable? One reason is that attorneys who lack experience often approach the sale of businesses the same way they approach court cases: fighting for every inch of ground they can to gain favor with their clients. I've witnessed, sadly enough, attorneys squabbling over the minutiae of the documents to gain ground while ignoring critical matters important to the seller. In these instances, I had to step in and steer the attorneys back on track to get the transaction closed.

This win/loss approach works well in a court case but fails miserably in a business acquisition. Attorneys are generally used to scrapping. They like to fight. They operate in a world where you fight and claw your way in the battle and get every advantage you possibly can, giving up nothing without a struggle. In their minds, winning is about gaining every possible advantage over your adversary that you possibly can through the process. Unfortunately, the wrong attorney will use these same tactics and approach the sale of a business in the same fashion as he or she is accustomed to, failing you miserably as your counsel.

The good news is that I will teach you how to set up metaphorical fences to ward off well-meaning transaction predators. You can still stumble through the legal phase of the sale without these fences, but believe me, it is a LOT easier if you follow the suggestions in this chapter. You want to be efficient, succinct, and thorough. You will also save money, time, and heartache by putting up fences to ward off well-meaning attorneys and CPAs.

Fence #1: Timing – Don't engage too early.

Don't engage your attorney too early in the transaction. This will help reduce unnecessary legal expenses and keep you on track without getting "out in the weeds." It is not necessary to hire an attorney before the letter of intent (LOI) stage of the transaction. If your LOI is nonbinding, you can rescind it at any time, so it isn't necessary to have your attorney look at it if you don't want to. The only important parts from a legal perspective are the binding provisions, which are usually confidentiality, exclusivity, business conduct, publicity, governing law, and working toward a closing.

Although not necessary, it is a good idea to have your attorney look at the binding provisions of the LOI to make sure you aren't getting into something you shouldn't. You need to understand what is binding and what is not. Hire your attorney to review the document *after* you have reached an agreement on the terms of the purchase with the buyer and are ready to execute the LOI—not before. Tell your attorney to take an hour to review it; don't let him or her burn up three hours for this task.

You will want your CPA to look at the LOI before executing it as well to make sure you understand the tax consequences and haven't missed anything pertinent to the taxes.

Fence #2: Taking Control – Don't just hand over the steering wheel.

This is the stage of the transaction where things can get out of control. You will need to take control from the start of the legal phase of the sale and maintain control throughout this process to the end. The approach and strategy are much different in a business sale than other transactions because of the relationship the buyer and seller will have post-closing. Since the buyer and seller will work together after the closing, it is optimal that they like each other and get along. The negotiation process must be fair. If buyer and seller carry battle wounds from the negotiations, they are less likely to get along after closing.

The single biggest factor in getting the seller paid is for the business to be profitable. The likelihood of the business being profitable is exponentially increased if the seller and buyer work together. Don't let the attorneys or CPAs crush this relationship. Taking control of this stage of the transaction is the way to accomplish this.

How do you take control?

Step 1: Have a call with the buyer to agree on the ground rules for the legal process. Here is a list of suggested ground rules:

- Treat this like a marriage, not a divorce. Buyer and seller need to work together afterward (the seller note will necessitate this), so there is a need to respect and protect the interests of each side. Remember, you can't intentionally poke your fiancé in the eye and expect him or her to be happy with you for it! Be considerate, play nice, and work together.

- No land grabs. This means there will be no adding additional provisions not previously agreed to by the buyer and seller.
- When revisions and comments are made, each one needs to have a reason for the changes being made so the other side can learn where they are coming from. If changes are made and you don't understand the reasoning behind the changes, misunderstandings can occur, causing undue grief.
- This is a "middle of the road" transaction, not a one-sided transaction. The documents are not to be one-sided but should protect both parties involved. Documents need to be fair to both parties.

Failure to set the ground rules in the beginning will cost you money and time and increase frustration, even make you angry. You could easily double your legal fees if you don't set ground rules and take control.

Step 2: Do an introductory call with attorneys from both sides and explain the ground rules you and the buyer already agreed to. Make sure the attorneys understand the rules and that both sides want to be mindful of unnecessary legal fees. Ask the attorneys to be mindful of the fees.

Fence #3: Getting Unstuck – Talk to your buyer and work for mutual benefit.

If you have a reasonable buyer, there are creative ways to work through problems. I've noticed that the best way to get past an impasse is to get the parties together and brainstorm to find solutions. It is helpful if one side will share and explain their perspective and reasoning behind their opinion first. Then the other side can share where they are coming from.

Getting past difficult terms often requires each side to give a little. Not everyone gets 100 percent of what they want all the time. Both sides may need to acquiesce in order to get the transaction done and negotiate a favorable outcome for both sides.

The best way to do this is to either do an in-person meeting or a phone call with you, the buyer, and your advisors. People are less likely to take a hard stance on the phone or in person than in an email. This call may or may not include your attorneys, depending on whether having them on the call would be helpful or not. Sometimes, it isn't helpful to have the attorneys on the call. You will need to use your best judgment with this.

The purpose of the call is to figure out a solution to the problem, so you will want to have the people who are best equipped to resolve the issue on this "getting unstuck" phone call. Recently, I was in the middle of the legal phase of a transaction in which we had some issues that needed to be resolved. We tried to resolve them with the attorneys on the phone, but the buyer's counsel kept trying to coerce him on the phone. Finally, we set up a call without the attorneys and came to terms.

Throughout the legal stage of the transaction, you must identify the things that are important. You will need to prioritize your needs. A good way to do so is to ask these two questions:

- What is the likelihood of the event happening?
- What is my exposure if it does happen?

If you are arguing over an issue that has a slim likelihood of happening and a small amount of exposure, perhaps it would be better to grant that item to the buyer and push hard on another issue that has a lot of exposure or high likelihood of occurrence. Once you prioritize your needs, it is easier to negotiate and work through issues. Sometimes you can give something to the buyer that costs you nothing but is important for the buyer to have. Not everything has the same priority—don't forget that. It is easy to get out in the weeds on nonissues that have a slim likelihood of ever happening. If solutions can't be reached, then it would be time to reach out to outside advisors who can give their input. Your M&A advisor or broker will be extremely valuable in this situation. This is where we earn our money.

Once you all agree on a solution, you can have the attorneys fix the documents to reflect the terms you agree to. I was once involved in a transaction in which a landlord hired an attorney to draft a lease agreement. The well-meaning attorney sought to make a land grab and changed the terms that were originally agreed upon. We had to push back on this issue, along with the landlord. When she found out about the land-grab, she wasn't happy.

If you have attorneys going rogue on you, I suggest having them on the call when you all agree to the terms of whatever issue you are trying to resolve. This lessens the chances of one person arbitrarily changing the terms of the agreement. They won't dare go rogue because they then have witnesses! It is unfortunate when this occurs because it wastes time and money for you and the buyer.

Bonus: Strategy

The best strategy to use when negotiating the sale of a business is to first identify and prioritize the most important issues associated with the sale and communicate these to your advisor and later to your attorney (in the legal phase of the transaction). I like using the old-fashioned list of A, B, or C items.

An A item is absolutely necessary or gives you the largest amount of exposure or potential future liability. These items are a must, and you need to get these negotiated in your favor at all costs. Since your A list is so important, you may give up several B and C items to get an A-list item.

B items are matters of importance, but not nearly as important as an A item. You can give up a B item for an A item, but not a C item.

C items are those you don't care too much about and which don't give you much exposure. For example, in the state of California, noncompete agreements aren't very enforceable. If you know this, you can allow the buyer to push hard on the term and distance of the noncompete agreement, since it isn't that important to you, and let the buyer "win" while you ask for a concession that is important to you.

Bonus: Negotiating Tactics

While you and your advisor negotiate, tackle small issues first before moving on to large issues. Give generously on small issues (C-list items) in the beginning; then you can hold back with important issues later. This strategy works for getting the important things you want and showing the buyer you are willing to work with him or her. You won't always get *everything you want*, but you will get the *main things* you want.

People want to work with people who are workable. Do not take "hard lines" on anything at first; wait to hear the other party's thoughts before making demands. Using your advisor during this phase is helpful for deflection. I've often been the one to take the blame for an issue and talk candidly to the buyer to protect the buyer–seller relationship moving forward. I can bring up an issue without having it hamper the seller's future ability to work with the buyer. This is where a third party comes in handy to carefully maneuver the transaction through treacherous territory.

Here are some good questions to ask yourself when considering a proposal:

- What is my risk?
- Am I willing to accept this risk?
- What do I give up if I accept the proposal? What do I gain?
- What is the likelihood this event will happen?
- What dollars would it cost?
- How important is this issue?

There may be times when you are willing to accept the risk and leave the documents alone. There may be other times you need to push hard due to risk and give up some other item that is less important. An old friend of mine once told me that if you ask for something, you need to be willing to give something up. That is the way the game is played. Be prepared to give something up when you ask for something. This is how it works.

CHAPTER 23

Choosing Your Advisory Team

As I write this book, I could not, in good conscience, let you go out on your own without helping you choose a good advisory team. Good advisors will be worth their weight in gold. They earn every dime you pay them. In this chapter, I will share my list of core principles that are vital for success. I will also share my list of trusted advisors as a starting point for you to assemble a good team. Finally, I will give you the tools and questions you need to ask potential selling advisors when interviewing them and selecting a good one to hire.

Core Principles

I've developed a list of inherent core principals of good advisors. This includes the principles they stand for and those they stand against.

Stand for

- Finding strategic buyers to maximize selling price
- Sellers paying lower taxes
- Accurate financial representation
- Being fair to all parties
- Maximum exposure to thousands of buyers (national and international)
- Maximum cash in your pocket
- Launching your business, not listing your business
- Selling by design, not by default
- Being honest, even when it hurts or is easier not to be

Stand against

- Untimely or premature entry to market
- Wasting people's time
- Deceit and deceitful practices
- Limited, one-sided seller representation
- Last minute "land grabs" to gain ground
- Renegotiating terms once they have been agreed upon
- Incompetence

Choosing the right advisors may also include letting go of the advisors you already have that are not a fit. For example, you may very well have outgrown your first accountant. Remember, your first accountant may not necessarily be your last accountant; being loyal to the wrong people can cost you big-time. For one of the single largest financial decisions of your life, you will need to dispose of underperforming people.

My List of Trusted Advisors

Against the behest of my legal advisor, I'm sharing a list of people I've worked with who stand for the set of principles I consider paramount to successful transactions. Although this is a good starting point, you will still need to interview people who are not on this list when considering hiring an advisor. Past performance is a good indicator of future performance, but not the only indicator. I don't take responsibility for their future actions, but I can tell you they stand for what I support and against that which I oppose. These people are true professionals.

Here is the list of my trusted advisors and their contact information, used with their permission. These people didn't ask to be included on the list. I wanted to include them to give you a starting point for your search.

Area of Expertise	Name	Firm	Website	Email
Transaction Attorney (>$10 million)	Russ Lombardy, II	Monarch Wealth Attorneys	monarchfirm.com	info@monarchfirm.com
Transaction Attorney	Simeon Vance	Parsons Behle & Latimer	parsonsbehle.com	SVance@parsonsbehle.com
	Brent J. Hawkins	Bennett, Tueller, Johnson & Deere	btjd.com	bhawkins@btjd.com
CAPS and Asset Exchange	Eric Veve	Epiquest Financial	assetexchangeexperts.com	eveve@epiqwest.com
CRT and CRUT (>$1 million)	Russ Lombardy, II	Monarch Wealth Attorneys	monarchfirm.com	info@monarchfirm.com
Charitable Gifting	Brock Bowden	Fortress Asset Management	fortressassetmanagement.com	brock@fortressam.com
Due Diligence	Andrew Averett	Upper Limit Consulting	upperlimitconsulting.com	andrew@upperlimitconsulting.com
ESOP & Life Insurance	Boyce Lowery	Suncrest Advisors	suncrestadvisors.com	boyce@suncrestadvisors.com
Life Insurance	Kira VanBree	Garda Insurance	gardainsurance.com	hello@gardainsurance.com
Cooperative Conversions	Amy Beres	Rocky Mountain Employer	rmeoc.org	info@rmeoc.org
Lending	John Briggs	Bank of the West	bankofthewest.com	John.Briggs@bankofthewest.com
	David Sherwood	Lend Base	lendbase.com	david@lendbase.com
Business Coach/Prep for Sale	Brandon Allen	New Work Revolution	newworkrevolution.com	brandon@newworkrevolution.com
	David Leis	Avantt Partners	avanttpartners.com	info@avanttpartners.com
Personal Finance/Prep for Sale	Garrett Gunderson	Wealth Factory	wealthfactory.com	Garrett.gunderson@wealthfactory.com
CPA (smaller size)	Brent King	Cheal King and Associates		bdkingcpapc@gmail.com
		Davies Allen	daviesallen.com	
CPA (medium size)	Anyone	Jones Simkins	jones-simkins.com	
		Cook Martin Poulson	cookmartin.com	
CPA (larger size)	Anyone	Tanner & Company	tannerco.com	

How to Choose an Advisory Team

The best way for me to help you choose your advisors is to give you a list of questions to ask in order to guide you through the process. I would suggest that you reach out to at least two people and interview both, then pick the best person for the job. Here are the questions you will want to consider:

Competition Comparison

- What makes the advisor stand out from the competition?
- What does he or she do better than the other people in the business?
- What is his or her formula for success?

Similarity

- How many similar transactions has the advisor done in the last 12 months?
- How much experience does the advisor have working on transactions of about the same size as your business?
- You will want to choose one who has experience with transactions that are of a similar size to yours. The reason for this is it takes a different skill set to sell and close a $150,000 pizza store than it does a $10 million logistics company.

Experience

- How many years has the advisor been working in this field?
- Does the advisor work full-time in the business?
- How many business sale transactions has the advisor closed in the last 12 months? It should be at least three.

References

- Ask for one or two references you can contact. Reach out to the references and ask them about their experience with the advisor. Make sure the references aren't family members.

Failures

- Ask about past failures and what the advisor learned.
- What are the reasons that transactions don't close?
- What percentage of listings don't sell?

Truth or Not?

- Is the advisor telling you the truth or what you want to hear?

Working Relationship

- Would you work well with this person?
- Do you see yourself getting along?
- Do you feel comfortable with this advisor?

Here are some additional questions specific to your broker, M&A advisor, or investment banker:

Strategic Buyers

- How does he or she find strategic buyers?
- What steps are necessary in order to get a good strategic buyer?

Market Timing

- What is the current market environment for selling a business?
- Is it a good time to sell?

Confidentiality

- How does he or she guard confidentiality?
- Is confidentiality important?

Industry Specialist

- Does your advisor have to specialize in selling your business type? Not necessarily. Remember the bakery sale I mentioned in Chapter 11: Types of Buyers You Will Encounter while Selling Your Business? Your best buyer may come from outside the industry you are in. If you hire an industry specialist, you are exposing your business to fewer buyers, which can mean a lower selling price. The one exception to this is dental practices; there are some industry specialists who do a great job selling only dental practices.

Marketing Plan

- How will he or she market your business?
- Does the advisor follow the *launch* philosophy or the *list* philosophy?

EPILOGUE

Now that I've given you all of the knowledge I can, you are ready to embark on the adventure of selling your business. It will be an experience like none you've ever had before, but you are now prepared for it. Hopefully, you can look back with pride after selling and say, "I built that, and now it belongs to someone else who will continue my legacy," as you sail off on the next chapter of your life doing what you love to do.

Who knows? You might even start another business after you get tired of golfing twice a day.

APPENDIX

Letter of Intent to Purchase

(Purchaser Name)
(Address)
(City, State Zip)
(Date)
Via Electronic Mail
(Seller Name)
(Address)
(City, State Zip) **(mention WORKING CAPITAL AND LEASES TO BE ASSUMED)**

Attn: [Name]

Dear **[Name]**:

The purpose of this letter of intent is to set forth the basic terms and conditions upon which **[Purchaser Name]** ("Purchaser") would acquire certain of the Assets and assume certain specified liabilities and obligations of **[Business Name]** ("Seller").

1. Assets to Be Acquired

The Assets to Be Acquired by Purchaser (the "Assets") shall consist of (i) substantially all tangible and intangible Assets owned or used by Seller in connection with the **[Name of Business Acquired]** identified on the attached Schedule A. Assets to include a Target Working Capital amount of $**[Number]**. The Selling Price shall be adjusted upward or downward for the Working Capital amount over or under the Working Capital Target.

2. Liabilities and Obligations to Be Assumed

Purchaser shall also assume liabilities at Closing as outlined in Schedule B (the "Liabilities Assumed"). Purchaser will assume all debts arising after Closing unless specifically excluded in the Purchase Agreement/Contract.

3. Purchase Price

The Purchase Price of the Assets shall be

1. $**[Number]**; plus
2. the Inventory Value, estimated to be $**[Number]**, to be determined within thirty (30) days of the Closing, by an inventory count conducted jointly by the parties.

The Purchase Price for the Assets shall be paid as follows:

- One (1) installment of $**[Number]** at Closing, of which $**[Number]** shall be paid from the amounts held in escrow and $**[Number]** of which shall be paid directly by the Buyer.
- The remaining balance shall be paid in **[Number Spelled Out]** (**[Number]**) equal installments on the annual anniversary date of the Closing (the "Installment Payments"). Interest shall accrue at **[Interest Rate]** percent per year.

4. Definitive Agreement Negotiations

As soon as practicable, the parties shall endeavor in good faith to enter definitive agreements to be executed at Closing, including, but not limited to, (i) the Purchase Agreement containing representations, warranties, covenants, conditions precedent, and indemnification provisions customary in transactions of the kind contemplated hereby and acceptable to both parties; (ii) the Noncompete Agreement; and (iii) the Lease Agreement.

5. Conduct of Business

Except as consented to by Purchaser, after execution of this letter of intent and until the Closing, (i) the business, affairs, and operations of Seller shall be conducted in a normal fashion and in a manner consistent with its methods of operation for prior periods; (ii) Seller shall not enter into any material commitment or incur any indebtedness or purchase or dispose of any material Assets other than in the ordinary course of business; and (iii) Seller shall not take any action which would frustrate the purpose of this letter of intent or the transactions provided for herein or contemplated hereby.

6. Due Diligence Review

Purchaser, directly and through its representatives, shall be afforded an opportunity to conduct such financial, legal, operating, and managerial Due Diligence Review of the Seller as it deems appropriate, and the results of such Due Diligence Review shall be satisfactory to Purchaser. The personnel and auditors and counsel of Seller shall cooperate with this Due Diligence Review.

7. Conditions

Consummation of the acquisition transactions provided for herein or contemplated hereby would be subject to certain conditions, including the following:

(a) Completion, to the satisfaction of Purchaser, of the Due Diligence Review provided for in paragraph 6 hereof.

(b) Approval by the parties of the definitive agreements, including the material terms set forth herein.

(c) Absence of any adverse change in the business or financial condition of Seller between the date of acceptance of this letter of intent by Seller and the Closing.

Purchase Price shall be contingent on Seller being able to substantiate the EBITDA/Cash Flow/SDE of $[Number].

(e) Seller shall provide training of [Number] hours for [Number] days at the business location and for an additional [Number] hours for [Number] days by phone consultation.

(f) Seller shall execute a Noncompete Agreement at Closing for a distance of **[Number]** miles and for **[Number]** years.

(g) Asset allocation shall be as outlined in Addendum C .

8. Confidentiality

Subject to paragraph 10 (Publicity) of this letter of intent, Seller and Purchaser agree that this letter of intent and all information disclosed during the course of negotiations and Purchaser's Due Diligence Review shall be held in confidence and shall not be disclosed to any third person (except their respective directors, officers, employees, accountants, attorneys, financial advisors, and other advisors on a "need to know" basis, provided that such persons agree not to disclose or use such information for any purpose except to evaluate the transactions provided for herein or contemplated hereby) and shall not be used for any purpose other than to evaluate the transactions provided for herein or contemplated hereby. In the event that the transactions contemplated by this Agreement do not close on or before **[Closing Date]**, all confidential information shall be returned to the party that furnished the confidential information, or destroyed, at the discretion of the disclosing party.

9. Exclusivity

In consideration for the considerable time, effort, and expense to be undertaken by Purchaser in connection with the transaction contemplated in this letter of intent, Seller agrees that (i) until **[Date (usually 60 days after signing this LOI)]**, Seller and its members shall negotiate exclusively with Purchaser and shall not undertake or continue acquisition discussions concerning the Assets described in Section 1 with any other party unless Purchaser agrees in writing; and (ii) Seller shall, in good faith, both timely respond to the due diligence requests of Purchaser and negotiate the terms of the definitive agreements in order to meet the Closing deadline of **[Closing Date]**.

In the event that Seller or Buyer determines to cancel this nonbinding letter of intent, it may do so with written notice at any time without penalty to either party.

10. Publicity

The parties shall consult with each other as to the form and substance of any press release or other public disclosure regarding the existence or terms of this letter of intent or the transactions provided for herein or contemplated hereby, and neither party shall make any public disclosure thereof prior to the Closing without the consent of the other.

11. Expenses

Seller shall bear the expenses which Seller and its members incur in connection with the transactions provided for herein or contemplated hereby, including the fees and expenses of its counsel and accountants and any fees and expenses of Seller's broker, and Purchaser shall bear the expenses which Purchaser incurs in connection with the transactions provided for herein or contemplated hereby, including the fees and expenses of its counsel, accountants, and any fees and expenses of Purchaser's broker.

12. Governing Law

This letter shall be governed by the internal laws of the State of **[Name of State]**, including its conflicts and choice of law provisions. This letter supersedes and shall control in the event of any conflict with the terms of this executed Confidentiality Agreement.

If this letter sets forth the general terms of the proposed transaction in a manner consistent with your understanding, kindly so indicate by signing on behalf of the Seller and returning to the undersigned the enclosed duplicate of this letter.

It is understood that this letter does not constitute a binding contract and that the parties do not intend to be legally bound until definitive agreements are executed by the parties; provided, however, that the parties agree to be legally bound by the provisions of paragraphs 4 (Definitive Agreement Negotiations), 5 (Conduct of Business), 6 (Due Diligence Review), 7 (Conditions), 8 (Confidentiality), and 9 (Exclusivity), which survive the termination of this letter and the abandonment of the transactions provided for herein or contemplated hereby, and paragraph 10 (Publicity), which shall be binding in accordance with its terms. This letter shall be withdrawn if not accepted by Seller before 5:00 p.m. **[Time Zone]** on **[Date]**.

Very truly yours,

[Name of Purchaser]

By: _____

Signature

Accepted and agreed to on this _____ day of **[Month]**, **[Year]**

[Name of Business]

By: _____

Signature of Seller

[Title of Seller]

Schedule A – List of Assets Acquired

This is a schedule of the assets to be included in the sale. It is usually provided by the Seller and included in the letter of intent.

Schedule B – List of Liabilities to be Assumed by Purchaser

This is a schedule of the debts that will be assumed by the Buyer.

Schedule C – Asset Allocation

The Purchase Price shall be allocated in the following manner:

$_____ Class I Assets – Cash

$_____ Class II Assets – Bonds and publicly traded stock

$_____ Class III Assets – Accounts receivable

$_____ Class IV Assets – Inventory

$_____ Class V Assets – Furniture, fixtures, equipment, buildings, and vehicles

$_____ Class VI Assets – Goodwill and noncompete agreement

$_____ Total Purchase Price

You can use IRS Form 8594 here as well. This form will need to be filed with the IRS after the sale of the business assets.

Sample Standard Nondisclosure Agreement

This Nondisclosure Agreement (the "Agreement"), effective as of the date last entered below (the "Effective Date"), is entered into by and between M&A Advisor Company, LLC (the "Disclosing Party"), and the Recipient named below (the "Recipient," and together with the Disclosing Party, the "Parties," and each, a "Party"). In connection with the consideration of a possible investment or financing transaction (the "Purpose"), the Recipient desires to receive certain information from the Disclosing Party that is nonpublic, confidential, or proprietary in nature. In consideration of the mutual covenants, terms, and conditions set forth herein, the Parties agree as follows:

1. Confidential Information

Except as set forth in Section 2 below, "Confidential Information" means all nonpublic, confidential, or proprietary information disclosed on or after the Effective Date, by the Disclosing Party to the Recipient or its affiliates, or to any of such Recipient's or its affiliates' employees, consultants, officers, directors, partners, shareholders, agents, attorneys, accountants, financing sources, or advisors (collectively, "Representatives"), however disclosed, including, without limitation,

(a) all information concerning the Disclosing Party's and its affiliates and their customers, employees, and suppliers, past, present, and future finances, customer information, supplier information, products, services, know-how, forecasts, business, marketing, development, sales, and other commercial strategies and the fact that the business is for sale;

(b) source and object code, programs, drawings, the Disclosing Party's unpatented inventions, ideas, methods and discoveries, trade secrets, unpublished patent applications, and other confidential intellectual property; and

(c) all notes, analyses, compilations, reports, studies, samples, data, statistics, summaries, interpretations, and other materials prepared by or for the Recipient or its Representatives that contain or derive from the foregoing and any other information that would reasonably be considered nonpublic, confidential, or proprietary given the nature of the information and the Parties' businesses.

2. Exclusions from Confidential Information

Except as required by applicable federal, state, or local law or regulation, the term "Confidential Information" as used in this Agreement shall not include information that

(a) at the time of disclosure is, or thereafter becomes, generally available to and known by the public other than as a result of, directly or indirectly, any act or omission by the Recipient or any of its Representatives;

(b) at the time of disclosure is, or thereafter becomes, available to the Recipient and its Representatives on a nonconfidential basis from a third-party source, provided that such third party is not and was not prohibited from disclosing such Confidential Information to the Recipient by any contractual obligation;

(c) was known by or in the possession of the Recipient or its Representatives, as established by documentary evidence, prior to being disclosed by or on behalf of the Disclosing Party pursuant to this Agreement;

(d) was or is independently developed by the Recipient or its Representatives, as established by documentary evidence, without reference to Confidential Information; or

(e) is Residual Information. "Residual Information" means the ideas, know-how, and techniques that would be retained in the unaided memory of an ordinary person skilled in the art, not intent on appropriating the proprietary information of the Disclosing Party, as a result of such person's access to, use, review, evaluation, or testing of the Confidential Information of the Disclosing Party for the purposes described herein. A person's memory is unaided if the person has not intentionally memorized the Confidential Information for the purpose of retaining and subsequently using or disclosing it. Nothing herein shall be deemed to grant to the Recipient a license under the Disclosing Party's intellectual property rights.

3. Recipient Obligations

The Recipient shall

(a) protect and safeguard the confidentiality of all Confidential Information with at least the same degree of care as the Recipient would protect its own confidential information, but in no event with less than a commercially reasonable degree of care;

(b) not use the Confidential Information, or permit it to be accessed or used, for any purpose other than the Purpose, including, without limitation, to reverse engineer, disassemble, decompile, or design around confidential intellectual property;

(c) not disclose any such Confidential Information to any person or entity, except to the Recipient's Representatives who need to know the Confidential Information in relation to the Purpose and are informed of the obligations hereunder and agree to abide by the same.

Recipient will promptly notify the Disclosing Party of any unauthorized disclosure of Confidential Information or other breaches of this Agreement.

4. Required Disclosure

Any Disclosure by the Recipient or its Representatives of any of the Disclosing Party's Confidential Information pursuant to applicable federal, state, or local law, regulation, or a valid order issued by a court or governmental agency of competent jurisdiction (a "Legal Order") shall be subject to the terms of this Section. Prior to making any such disclosure, the Recipient shall make commercially reasonable efforts to provide the Disclosing Party with

(a) prompt written notice of such requirement so that the Disclosing Party may seek a protective order or other remedy; and

(b) reasonable assistance in opposing such disclosure or seeking a protective order or other limitations on disclosure.

If, after providing such notice and assistance as required herein, the Recipient remains subject to a Legal Order to disclose any Confidential Information, the Recipient (or its Representatives or other persons to whom such Legal Order is directed) shall disclose only that portion of the Confidential Information which, on the advice of the Recipient's legal counsel, such Legal Order specifically requires.

5. Return or Destruction of Confidential Information

Upon the expiration or termination of this Agreement, or at the Disclosing Party's request at any time during the term of this Agreement, the Recipient and its Representatives shall promptly return to the Disclosing Party all copies, whether in written, electronic, or other form or media, of the Disclosing Party's Confidential Information, or destroy all such copies and confirm the same in writing to the Disclosing Party, provided that the Recipient and its Representatives may retain such Confidential Information as is necessary to enable it to comply with its reasonable document-retention policies.

6. Term and Termination

The term of this Agreement shall commence on the Effective Date and shall expire 18 months from the Effective Date, provided that either Party may terminate this Agreement at any time by providing written notice to the other Party. Notwithstanding anything to the contrary herein, each Party's rights and obligations under this Agreement, irrespective of termination of this Agreement, shall survive until the 18-month anniversary of this Agreement, even after the return or destruction of Confidential Information by the Recipient (the "Confidential Period"), provided that for any and all trade secrets of the Disclosing Party, the Confidential Period shall last for as long as such Confidential Information qualifies as a trade secret under applicable federal, state, and/or local law.

7. No Transfer of Rights, Title, or Interest

The Disclosing Party hereby retains its entire right, title, and interest, including all intellectual property rights, in and to all Confidential Information.

8. No Other Obligation

The Parties agree that this Agreement does not require or compel the Disclosing Party to disclose any Confidential Information to the Recipient or obligate any Party to enter into a business or contractual relationship. Either Party may terminate discussions at any time.

9. Remedies

The Recipient acknowledges and agrees that money damages might not be a sufficient remedy for any breach or threatened breach of this Agreement by the Recipient or its Representatives. Therefore, in addition to all other remedies available at law, the Disclosing Party shall be entitled to seek specific performance and injunctive and other equitable relief as a remedy for any such breach or threatened breach, and the Recipient hereby waives any requirement for the securing or posting of any bond or the showing of actual monetary damages in connection with such claim.

10. Nonsolicitation and Noncircumvention

During the term of this Agreement and for a period of twelve (12) months after the expiration or termination of this Agreement, without the Disclosing Party's prior written consent, the Recipient and its Representatives shall not contact or solicit an employee of the Disclosing Party for the purpose of hiring them, solicit the business of any client, customer, or licensee of the Disclosing Party, or, outside of the ordinary course of business, directly or indirectly contact or participate in communications with any disclosed companies, entities, or persons (including each of their affiliates, parents, or subsidiaries). Notwithstanding anything to the contrary herein, the Recipient and its Representatives shall not be restricted from hiring any employee of Disclosing Party who responds to a general solicitation for employment not directed toward the Disclosing Party's employees.

11. Governing Law, Jurisdiction, and Venue

This Agreement shall be governed by and construed in accordance with the internal laws of the State of Utah without giving effect to any choice or conflict of law provision or rule that would cause the application of Laws of any jurisdiction other than those of the State of Utah. Any legal suit, action, or proceeding arising out of or related to this Agreement or the matters contemplated hereunder shall be instituted exclusively in the federal courts of the United States or the courts of the State of Utah.

12. Notices

All notices, requests, consents, claims, demands, waivers, and other communications hereunder shall be in writing by email and shall be deemed to have been given on the date sent by email if sent during normal business hours of the Recipient and on the next business day if sent after normal business hours of the Recipient to the email address provided by the parties at the time hereof.

13. Miscellaneous

This Agreement constitutes the sole and entire agreement of the Parties with respect to the subject matter hereof and supersedes all other understandings and agreements with respect to such subject matter. If any term hereof is invalid or unenforceable, it shall not affect any other term or provision of this Agreement. Neither Party may assign this Agreement without written consent of the other Party. No waiver shall be deemed or implied hereunder.

IN WITNESS WHEREOF, the parties have executed this Agreement to be effective as of the Effective Date.

RECIPIENT

Company Name (if applicable): _____

Your Name: _____

Date: _____

Email: _____

Phone: _____

Business in Which You Are Interested: _____

Signature: _____

Sample Due Diligence Checklist

- ☐ Revenue Recognition Practices
  - ☐ Description of how revenue is recorded, recognized, and earned
  - ☐ Are there any customer discounts? If so, how much and how does that work?
  - ☐ Suppliers (list of)
  - ☐ Suppliers (contracts)
  - ☐ All supplier contracts, including amounts, length of the contract, and provisions for default
  - ☐ Listing of all vendors/suppliers and dollars spent in the past 12 months
- ☐ Cash
  - ☐ 2019, 2018, and 2017 bank statements, all business accounts
  - ☐ Bank reconciliations for 2019, 2018, and 2017
- ☐ Accounts Receivable
  - ☐ List of AR
  - ☐ Aging for AR as of 12/31/18 and most recent for 2019
- ☐ Financials
  - ☐ Annual cash flow statements for fiscal year 2018–2017, if you have them
  - ☐ Annual balance sheet and income statements for 2017, 2018, and YTD 2019
  - ☐ YTD balance sheet and income statements for 2019
- ☐ Taxes
  - ☐ Federal tax returns for 2018, 2017, and 2016
  - ☐ State tax returns for 2018, 2017, and 2016
  - ☐ Sales tax reports for 2019, 2018, and 2017
  - ☐ Personal property returns for 2018 and 2017 (if applicable)
- ☐ Business Licenses and Permits
  - ☐ Copies of all business licenses and permits as of today

- [ ] Schedule of all business licenses
- [ ] **Threatened or Pending Litigation**
  - [ ] A list of all threatened or pending litigation and government orders
  - [ ] Copies of all correspondence related to the claims
  - [ ] Names and phone numbers of attorneys who are handling
- [ ] **Related Party Transactions**
  - [ ] List of all related parties and description of transactions with them
- [ ] **Employee Benefits**
  - [ ] List of employee benefits
  - [ ] Copies of all insurance paperwork, 401(k) plan paperwork, and employee benefit plans
  - [ ] Information about any labor disputes
- [ ] **Insurance**
  - [ ] Copy of liability policy

Insurer	Type of Insurance	Policy #	Insured	Coverages	Amount of Coverage	Deductible

  - [ ] Copy of health insurance plan
  - [ ] Copy of any other insurance you may have in place
  - [ ] Copy of all insurance certificates
  - [ ] See Insurance Data Request List
- [ ] **Accounts Payable**
  - [ ] A detailed list of AP and AP aging as of 12/31/18 and as of today
- [ ] **Workers' Comp**
  - [ ] Copies of all workers' comp filings for 2017, 2018, and 2019
  - [ ] Copies of any findings from WC audits, if any

- ☐ Indebtedness
    - ☐ List of all debts

Debtor	Amount Due	Monthly Payment	Years Remaining

    - ☐ Copies of all notes and debt agreements
    - ☐ See Template for Schedule of Indebtedness
- ☐ Customers
    - ☐ List of all customer contracts
    - ☐ Revenue for 2017, 2018, and YTD 2019 by customer (with names blocked out if you'd like)—customer concentration
    - ☐ Copies of all customer contracts
- ☐ Equity
    - ☐ List of owners and their percentage of ownership
    - ☐ Minutes of all meetings and copies of all written consents of the board of directors and the committees thereof of the company and any subsidiaries for the last five years ownership structure
    - ☐ Any stockholder agreements, voting trusts, proxy agreements, escrow agreements, or similar arrangements
    - ☐ Phantom stock/incentive plan details if any
    - ☐ Salaries and bonuses for senior management for fiscal years 2016–current
- ☐ Permits and Licenses
    - ☐ List and copies of all permits and licenses
    - ☐ Any other material governmental qualifications, registrations, business licenses, permits, authorizations, exemptions, or security clearances pursuant to federal, state, or provincial regulations

- ☐ All other registrations needed to conduct business in each country, province, state, etc.
- ☐ Partnerships and Subsidiaries
  - ☐ List of all wholly-owned subsidiaries and all partnerships, joint ventures, or limited liability companies in which the company has an interest (collectively, the "subsidiaries"), detail of the company ownership, and copies of all constituent documents of the subsidiaries (e.g., certificate or articles of incorporation, bylaws, etc.)
  - ☐ List of all other partnerships, joint ventures, or limited liability companies in which the company has less than a 100 percent interest
  - ☐ Copies of all related joint venture or strategic alliance agreements
- ☐ Products
  - ☐ Breakdown of revenue by revenue type for fiscal years 2018 YTD–2017
  - ☐ Services rendered, pricing policies, and procedures
  - ☐ Sales and gross profit by type of service provided
- ☐ Sales and Marketing
  - ☐ Description of fulfillment process: typical process and time frame from contract to delivery to customers
  - ☐ Any relevant information on order backlog or committed volumes
  - ☐ Sales pipeline, including target customers, product type, sales volume potential, probability, and timing
  - ☐ Marketing brochures, catalogs, and other product literature
- ☐ Real Estate
  - ☐ List of facilities, including address, square feet of office, and description
  - ☐ Description of facilities and plants, including a listing of all material fixed assets and accumulated depreciation (This can be the depreciation schedule.)

- ☐ Available appraisal for any equipment
- ☐ Safety records if available
- ☐ Estimated total capacity and current utilization
- ☐ Copies of real estate leases
- ☐ List of RE leases, expiration dates, and terms
- ☐ List of any leased real property, including descriptions, terms of leases, and sale, as well as leaseback arrangements, options, annual costs, etc.
- ☐ Equipment
  - ☐ Estimated average age of the equipment
  - ☐ Acquisitions during 2017, 2018, and 2019
  - ☐ Dispositions during 2017, 2018, and 2019
  - ☐ Capitalization policy
  - ☐ List of fixed assets (depreciation schedule)
  - ☐ Summary of CAPEX for the past 24 months and future 12 months.
- ☐ Computer System (Hardware and Software)
  - ☐ Copies of leases for software
  - ☐ Description of the internal computer system(s), including accounting, inventory tracking, and data processing systems
- ☐ Employees
  - ☐ List of employees

Employee	Pay Rate	Time with Company	Position/ Title	PT or FT	Benefits? (Y/N)

- ☐ Organizational chart
- ☐ Copies of noncompete agreements with employees

- ☐ All employee contracts
- ☐ Employee manuals and handbooks

☐ Industry and Competition

- ☐ List of major competitors in the area with a discussion of how the company differentiates from each
- ☐ List of all tradeshows, industry events, and industry organizations in which the company participates
- ☐ Monthly Contracts to be Assumed for Leased Equipment

☐ Ongoing Contracts

- ☐ List of ongoing contracts that will need to be assumed with terms for each

Contract	Monthly Payment	Description	Time Left on Contract	Early Buyout Penalty

Made in the USA
Columbia, SC
14 February 2022

55887832R00109